HOW DO I TALK TO MY KIDS ABOUT SOCIAL JUSTICE?

HOW DO I TALK TO MY KIDS ABOUT SOCIAL JUSTICE?

Protecting Your Kids From the Woke Indoctrination of Public Schools.

CHUCK MASON, MDIV

XULON ELITE

Xulon Press Elite
2301 Lucien Way #415
Maitland, FL 32751
407.339.4217
www.xulonpress.com

© 2023 by Chuck Mason, MDiv

All rights reserved solely by the author. The author guarantees all contents are original and do not infringe upon the legal rights of any other person or work. No part of this book may be reproduced in any form without the permission of the author.

Due to the changing nature of the Internet, if there are any web addresses, links, or URLs included in this manuscript, these may have been altered and may no longer be accessible. The views and opinions shared in this book belong solely to the author and do not necessarily reflect those of the publisher. The publisher therefore disclaims responsibility for the views or opinions expressed within the work.

Unless otherwise indicated, Scripture quotations taken from the Holy Bible, New International Version (NIV). Copyright © 1973, 1978, 1984, 2011 by Biblica, Inc.™. Used by permission. All rights reserved.

Paperback ISBN-13: 978-1-6628-6874-0
Ebook ISBN-13: 978-1-6628-6875-7

Acknowledgments

God willing, this book is the first of many I'll write, but it wasn't possible without the assistance of people who attended my seminars on the many and various postmodern deconstructions of our culture and encouraged me to create a resource for parents and people who are at a loss to challenge social justice narratives. There's the phrase, people want to be writers, but few want to write. It's accurate; writing's a painful process for most. I took their advice and endured the pain, paying them back by asking them to review my work to see if it had the merit they perceived. They did, and their feedback, helpful in all respects, unknowingly became my motivation to find time away from work and my sons to complete this project. One never knows the impact any book will have, but I do know this book wouldn't exist without them. So, I thank Rob, Russ, and Heidi Jo for your valuable time, careful consideration, and encouragement. And most of all, I thank Tim for your efforts toward seeing this book published. To those who read, if this work has been a help and blessing to you and your family, please pray for us all.

Table of Contents

CHAPTER 1
It's Indoctrination, and It's Intentional. 1

CHAPTER 2
You Speak Facts; They Speak Emoji. 9

CHAPTER 3
The Time You Spend Together Makes the Difference 29

CHAPTER 4
Kindergarten Drag Queen Story Hour 37

CHAPTER 5
Your Child Is a Young White (or White Adjacent) Supremacist 55

CHAPTER 6
Conform or Be Cast Out 79

CHAPTER 7
Perspectives 89

Introduction

In January 1993, I found myself admiring the San Gabriel Mountains from a campus balcony while I was on a class break from biblical Greek. I was pursuing a Master of Divinity degree from Fuller Theological Seminary, and as I admired those mountains, I knew I had to be there, but I had no idea what I was going to do. During the 1990s, Fuller provided the world's best pastoral training, but I had zero interest in becoming a pastor. The role of a pastor is a specific calling, and I knew then, as I know now, that I wanted nothing to do with the responsibility of shepherding souls from cradle to grave. I separated myself from the suit and pulpit like Jonah separated himself from Nineveh. Yet there I was pursuing a Fuller MDiv, the gold standard for conservative pastoral training, without any idea what I would do when I graduated.

The degree came with its challenges; it was as expensive as a law degree, took just as long to complete, and ultimately left me without a career path. I learned how to become a business owner and entrepreneur overnight. But my time at Fuller began a journey down a long and winding road that led me to postmodern philosophy and this book, *How Do I Talk to my Kids about Social Justice?*

The MDiv program required a class on philosophy. I don't remember the class title, but I'll never forget stumbling into postmodern philosophy, its attack on truth, and the terrifying reality it created for our world. I was stunned by the audacity of postmodernity's goal to undermine every concept of truth and the authority of the Judeo-Christian worldview. It was determined to deconstruct the modern world and American society. I was shocked by the temerity of the movement but realized postmodern criticisms of the modern world had significant points; the movement could achieve these goals over time, which had chilling consequences for humanity. A deconstructed civilization that rejects concepts of truth rejects the principles that order society and constrain human behavior. When these decay, society devolves into chaos. *Lord of the Flies* was written for a reason.

I spent the rest of my program taking as many classes on philosophy and culture as possible, which led to an intellectual life dedicated to tracking the cultural carnage of postmodernity. The woke narratives of social justice are the latest wave of philosophical thought that continues to drink from postmodernity's poisoned well. I've dedicated my intellectual life to educating and raising the alarm about the direction of American culture over the past decades and holding countless forums challenging the central themes of postmodern philosophy and moral relativism, individual perspectives on truth, LGBTQ, critical race theory, and cancel culture. Over the years, the response was mixed at best, and people were indifferent due to their inability to understand ideas that hadn't fully emerged in culture. Their lives hadn't been negatively impacted because the philosophy hadn't hit the comfort of their homes. Liberals, moderates, conservatives, Christians, and people of other faiths have been able to retreat to their preferred cultural spaces, avoiding the impact of postmodernity. All that has changed; woke narratives and social justice are transforming our kids. Woke has brought the battle to our homes.

Our kids can't hide; social justice narratives are force-fed to our children through intentional indoctrination in our public schools. They're becoming woke and embracing narratives that are as indefensible as they are unimaginable. As parents, we feel helpless, not knowing what to do. I watched the woke culture impact my sons, which was devastating, especially for me. I had the perfect training to combat this in my home, but I reacted out of fear and frustration. Reacting never works. I finally took a step back and came to terms with my approach; I needed to stop responding like a parent and apply my education to my sons. I did, and it worked. I developed, *How Do I Talk to my Kids about Social Justice* as a series of forums to share these highly effective methods. Several close friends said these forums needed to become a book as a resource for parents, and here we are.

There are several things to remember as you take this journey to combat social justice and protect your kids. Social justice narratives are the product of the significant transformations of philosophy and moral theory that emerged from the postmodern deconstruction of knowledge and American culture. They can only be well understood by comprehending the processes that created them. Trust me when I say that regurgitating a few trite talking points will get you nowhere in challenging these narratives. They're the product of over a century of intellectual development, and you must understand the story if you're going to protect your kids. I'll take you on the journey of ideas to know how we got here and how we move forward. It's not as painful as you might think; those who approach this with an open mind find it fascinating. If you're wondering how the world has lost its mind, you'll understand the motivation behind the radical policies that are deconstructing society right before our eyes when you've finished reading.

I talk about the basic themes of philosophy and epistemology (the theory of knowledge) here in very basic terms that every reader can understand. I haven't cluttered most of this book with endless references and citations about the Enlightenment, Marxism, or postmodernity. Internet searches quickly confirm my descriptions and characterizations of these philosophical movements. I did choose to document my analysis of critical race theory. Given the rhetoric and violence that stems from groups such as BLM and Antifa that hold the theory in high esteem, I thought it necessary to back my claims with research from leading minority scholars. The next book, which I'll have started by the time you're reading this, will cover all the major intellectual transformations in depth with quotes, citations, and analysis.

Those trained in philosophy might find this book oversimplified, but that is intentional. I make no effort to present a thorough epistemology here; I'm merely a cultural observer describing people's choices as they try to comprehend reality and order society. For the most part, humanity doesn't care about technical philosophy, and I don't blame them (I wonder if anyone truly understands Kant or Derrida). Praxis rarely adheres to theory; people do as they wish, often without knowing why. If you're critical of my analysis in any way, contact me through my website at www.battlegroundideas.com, and you can take issue with me there.

As it turns out, my aversion to the pastorate was an accurate read of a still, small voice leading me in a direction I couldn't recognize. The journey has been interesting. I tried to warn congregations about what was coming, but people entrenched in the comfort of American life couldn't understand until their kids sat through Drag Queen Story Hour. Decades later, it all makes sense, yet I have one regret: I should have put more energy into my efforts over the years. Knowing this, I am sharing my journey with you so we can take the battle of protecting our kids to a new level.

> "Trust in the LORD with all your heart and lean not on your own understanding; in all your ways submit to him, and he will make your paths straight" (Prov. 3:5–6 NIV).

Trust your intuition as you engage this culture. The situation is dire, and our kids are at risk, but there is power in truth that God reveals at every turn. Take what you learn from this book and protect your children and America. Know this, the battle may belong to the Lord, but He entrusted you to wage the cultural fight. Get up and get in the game; your children need you. Blessings . . .

CHAPTER 1

It's Indoctrination, and It's Intentional

Woke, LGBTQ, white privilege, gender fluid, non-binary, preferred pronouns, implicit bias, critical race theory . . . welcome to the social justice vocabulary of your children, compliments of their public school "education," an education that is an indoctrination into a worldview that mainstreams Marxism and leaves parents feeling helpless. We send our kids to schools, handing them over to teachers and administrators who smile and say, "Don't worry, they're in good hands. Kindergarten Drag Queen Story Hour frees your five-year-old from their intolerant transphobic Judeo-Christian bigotry. Restorative justice transforms your child. Trust us, and trust the system. Comply, or your name gets added to the FBI domestic terrorist watch list."

This isn't a dystopian adaptation of Orwell's *1984*, updated to the twenty-first century. It's your reality, your child's reality in America today. It's incomprehensible that schools serve as agents for our children's progressive transformation, forcing a worldview openly hostile to America and the Judeo-Christian foundations of society. But that's the state of America, and our kids are caught in the middle, intentional targets for reeducation in a culture war that fights for the future of America. Schools are ground zero in a battle for the hearts and minds of our kids, indoctrination centers for woke culture, and it's intentional. Teachers, administrators, and school board members purposefully choose curriculums that present social justice narratives as sacrosanct truth, excluding other perspectives, especially the traditional American worldview, from the classroom.

This is the classic example of indoctrination, teaching someone to uncritically accept a set of beliefs without offering or allowing counter viewpoints. Classrooms present a singular perspective, and kids face a difficult choice: embrace social justice narratives or face cancel culture, confess their white privilege, or fail. This was intentional; teachers and administrators made it hard to uncover because they knew you'd never accept it. You'd never knowingly accept the indoctrination of your kids because you knew the effect it would have on them. The indoctrination has a heartbreaking impact.

According to Barna Group,[1] nearly two out of three teens and young adults leave the faith and common-sense values when they graduate high school and transition to the university and their careers. They feel traditional American and biblical perspectives cannot relate to the challenge of progressive concepts of gender fluidity, sexual identity, sexual practice, and racial and economic justice. Social justice narratives provide a new form of morality,

---

[1] "Church Dropouts Have Risen To 64%-But What About Those Who Stay?" Barna Group, 2019, https://www.barna.com/research/resilient-disciples/.

giving them the justification they need to break from a Judeo-Christian worldview to explore lifestyles of their choice. They reject faith, families, traditional perspectives, and common sense as they embark on a journey of complete self-determination. Kids flex their wings when they leave home, unable to realize they become like Icarus racing toward a woke ideology that can burn like the sun.

As parents, it's unimaginable; we feel entirely powerless, not knowing what to do or how to challenge indoctrination. I know because I lived this. I had two sons in public school, and I watched them embrace social justice narratives as peer pressure, cancel culture, and emotional appeals to tolerance and fairness had a profound effect. I reacted out of fear, attempting to push them out of the indoctrination with rational arguments and frustration, which drove them further into woke culture. This led me to develop the insights I am sharing with you. I decided to use my education and years of public speaking about postmodern culture to establish this method using the knowledge and resources I gained from studying postmodern philosophy and culture at Fuller Theological Seminary. I've been challenging critical race theory, LGBTQ, and cancel culture for years, and I've used all my resources to help you protect your kids. This method gives you the information, tools, and resources you need to protect your kids against social justice indoctrination.

It's important to understand that the indoctrination of kids is a part of the dramatic and comprehensive philosophical battle over the ideas that shape and influence the heart and soul of America. This is a fight to decide whether concepts of morality,

God, science, and truth exist and how they affect the cultural institutions of society. There are two opposing worldviews—traditional American and post-truth Marxism—battling for our culture. Everything is in play. The Conservative Right wants to preserve traditional America and its Christian heritage. The Progressive Left intends to deconstruct America, indoctrinating kids with a morality that conforms to Marxist social justice principles using LGBTQ and critical race theory concepts. This is a fight to determine the organizing principles of our country, whether they will be freedom guided by the Judeo-Christian worldview or Marxism that demands obedience to social justice. The foundations of America's cultural institutions are at risk, and the reeducation of our kids is a critical part of an agenda the Left has been advancing for decades in our school systems.

Soccer moms, Conservatives, Independents, classic Liberals, and Christians couldn't see or didn't want to see the transformation happening before our eyes. Covid revealed how deeply social justice narratives transformed public schools. We were shocked when health officials sent our kids home, and online education drew the curtain back to see the principles of critical race theory and LGBTQ dominating our kid's curriculums. Ideological Marxists were pulling the levers of public education. They told us to pay no mind to the man behind the curtain, but it was too late to unsee the little shop of horrors they created: white privilege, gender fluidity, biological boys accessing girl's locker rooms, Drag Queen Story Hour, family defined as hetero-normal binary oppression, and the casting of America as a country so inherently racist from

IT'S INDOCTRINATION, AND IT'S INTENTIONAL

its inception that it's beyond saving. These narratives inform every subject in schools, from English to science. It was intentional, culminating in a plan that had been decades in the making.

Progressives have wanted to purge the influence of Christianity from society for nearly a century. They want an America that's free, open, and tolerant, but the "bigotry" of the Judeo-Christian worldview stands in their way. Biblical principles have been the basis of America's social fabric and legal system since its founding. People may not have considered themselves Christians or sought a relationship with Christ, but they have recognized the unique freedom and prosperity the influence these principles provide. Yet, the embrace of the Judeo-Christian worldview and its biblical heritage was never ubiquitous, and an ever-growing Progressive movement fought to move the country beyond its biblical influences. Although deeply flawed, the intellectual revolution of the postmodern movement gave Progressives the justification they needed to purge Christianity's influence from the land. America's education system became ground zero for the fight. Can you imagine a better scenario to establish counterfactual narratives and reeducate generations of Americans than public schools? Impressionable young minds are held captive for seven hours each day, naively absorbing whatever narratives they're given. It's a perfect scenario to reorder their thinking. Kids are like intellectual sheep sent to ideological slaughter.

The fact that schools have become indoctrination centers for societal transformation shouldn't surprise us. As the sixties' radicals became the majority faculty at universities, they graduated generations of Americans who fully embraced the postmodern attack on truth and the narrative that America was a racist, bigoted, patriarchal, homophobic, and transphobic nation that needed to be transformed. These university grads became the ever-growing percentage of postmodern Progressives who wanted to purge traditional America of its Judeo-Christian influence and build a society based on tolerance, fairness, and equity. They are quietly our neighbors, children's teachers, school administrators, and the people elected to our school board because we ignored local elections. They brought their postmodern vision of a Progressive America in tow to right the wrongs of America's history by reeducating our kids with an emerging post-truth Marxist worldview.

The transformation took generations, and for the most part, we didn't engage in the fight for our kids. Conservatives reacted with, at best mild indignation, and bemusement that university radicals would even try to mainstream anti-America views. Christians retreated to their churches claiming the comfortable myth that God, in His providence, unilaterally preserves nations founded on the principles of His Word. Independents and classic Liberals all saw tolerance and fairness as good if it was practiced in moderation, ignoring the obvious that sixties radicals despised moderation, especially those who preached the gospel of Marxism. We all missed the painful reality that societies, even societies built on biblical principles, reap the peril of neglecting school board elections. Progressives quietly advanced their agenda year after year.

We've lost a lot of cultural ground; there's no denying that, but all is not lost. You can protect your children (and challenge

IT'S INDOCTRINATION, AND IT'S INTENTIONAL

your school boards) if you're willing to recognize that your kids are caught in a philosophical battle for America. It's a battle of ideas. To win, you'll have to take a short intellectual journey to realize what this battle is all about. This involves understanding how you comprehend reality using a traditional American worldview that relies on critical thinking and Judeo-Christian principles, how your kids are being reeducated to comprehend reality with a post-truth Marxist worldview using their emotions guided by Marxism, and the tools you'll need to bridge the gap. You can't argue them out of the indoctrination using logic and frustration. I know because I tried. I learned that you could challenge your kids to examine facts and face the ideological failures found in critical race theory, LGBTQ ideals, and cancel culture. They're intellectually unsustainable once challenged and a nightmare once implemented in society. Teens haven't wholly abandoned critical thinking; they understand these flawed ideologies impact culture and their lives. There is hope if you're willing to learn how these ideologies developed, how they work, and how they're used to reeducate kids.

There's a learning process involved, but it can't be avoided if you're going to protect them effectively. This Pandora's box of ideologies wasn't opened overnight. They're the product of more than a century of intellectual development. It's impossible to challenge them without having intelligent conversations. If you don't understand how they work, you'll react out of fear and ignorance, leading to heated discussions on the road to nowhere. That's why you feel helpless, not sure where to turn. When people don't have the tools and information to make credible intellectual challenges, they react out of frustration and anger. This is precisely why frantic parents react at school board meetings attacking the presence of CRT in curriculums, male "trans-athletes" destroying girls' athletics, and Kindergarten Drag Queen Story Hour. The National School Board Association requested the Biden administration paint them as enraged domestic terrorists, ignorant bigots who hate minorities and trans kids.[2] The Progressive Left will wage this propaganda war if parents react out of emotion because of a lack of understanding. The battle for your kids can't be won without education on your part, and it's a battle you can win.

If you're ready, turn the page, and we can start the journey to protecting your kids right now.

---

[2] Timothy H.J. Nerozzi, "States sue Biden admin over FBI surveillance of parents protesting school boards," New York Post, March 4, 2022, https://nypost.com/2022/03/04/states-sue-biden-admin-over-fbi-surveillance-of-parents-protesting-school-boards/.

CHAPTER 2

You Speak Facts; They Speak Emoji

Try talking with your kids using facts and logic today; the odds are you won't get very far. They're conditioned to reject critical thinking and rely on their feelings to dictate "reality." It's part of a process that introduces them to an entirely new way of interpreting the world. Kids are conditioned to use their feelings to determine what is "real." Relying on emotions conditions them to embrace emotionally-driven narratives portraying America as a systemically racist society built on the oppression, exploitation, and victimization of women, minorities, the LGBTQ community, and the poor. This is the grievance lens of Marxism, causing kids to adopt a new moral system to determine what is acceptable in society. Public education is indoctrinating kids, and it's entirely intentional.

Kids are caught in a polarizing battle to determine how America comprehends reality and organizes society. This fight has two sides with opposing worldviews: traditional America versus post-truth Marxist America. They use incompatible methods to determine reality (critical thinking versus emotions) and moral systems to decide what they will and won't accept in society (Judeo-Christianity versus Marxism). It's a fight to define our culture's fundamental principles, and Progressives in public schools are intentionally reeducating children. Whoever controls public education profoundly influences a generation's worldview, and as each generation matures and votes, it ultimately controls politics and culture. Kids are ground zero in the culture war, and their indoctrination is a deliberate attempt by Progressives to transform America one impressionable mind at a time.

The indoctrination of your children has two main themes. First, they're conditioned to reject logic and critical thinking, relying instead on their feelings and emotions to analyze the world. Second, they are taught to evaluate the world through a new moral system, Marxist social justice. Together, these provide a comprehensive method to determine what is "real" and what is ethical and just for society. I'm calling this comprehensive method post-truth Marxism, and it's the ideological driving force behind the development of the social justice narratives of critical race theory, LGBTQ, and cancel culture. It's also completely reordering how your kids think, making it nearly impossible to reason with them.

This is precisely why we have difficulty communicating with our children. We analyze the world through facts, data, logic, and critical thinking; your kids use feelings, emotions, and preferences. We rely on the guidance of the Judeo-Christian worldview to inform our moral decisions. They rely on the Marxist victimization narratives of social justice to decide what is right. When it comes to conversations with your kids, you come with data, and they come with feelings. You speak facts; they speak emoji.

If you're concerned for your kids, you are embracing a traditional American worldview, a method of understanding the world that opposes nearly everything your children are indoctrinated with. Traditional America is a product of an intellectual revolution called the Enlightenment, which relied on logic and rational thought to analyze the world and Judeo-Christian principles to guide the creation of a society built on freedom and personal responsibility. Your children are indoctrinated with a post-truth Marxist worldview that teaches them to use their feelings to analyze the world and the principles of Marxism to guide them as they create new laws and a new society built on the principles of social justice. Traditional America and Marxism have never been able to coexist anywhere in the world; each has tried to eradicate the other whenever they conflict. That's why it's nearly impossible to talk with kids; they're being given a worldview and moral system openly hostile to everything that has come before in traditional America.

Kids are indoctrinated with a post-truth Marxist perspective that sees America as an oppressive, exploitative country that must be transformed into a society based upon social justice and Marxist equity. Critical race theory, LGBTQ ideals, and cancel culture are manifestations of social justice within society. This message is the central theme of your child's public education, which is continually reinforced. Drag Queen Story Hours are a lived reality of this worldview with a purpose. We see Kindergarten Drag Queen Story Hour and wonder how the world lost its mind. The Progressive

Left sees drag queens as an effective tool to teach a five-year-old to unquestioningly accept socially conditioned sexuality (don't let anyone tell you this isn't indoctrination). Drag Queen Story Hour is the manifestation of a post-truth Marxist worldview being forced upon your kids.

How you respond is essential. If you react to drag queens out of anger, you lose sight of the larger picture, that your children are caught in a battle between two antithetical worldviews about the nature of reality and morality. To protect your kids, you must understand how each worldview works to communicate strategies that effectively challenge the ideas behind indoctrination. We're going to take a short journey through the history of philosophy (don't worry, it's fascinating) to understand these different perspectives, the indoctrination your kids are receiving, and how we bridge the gap.

The battle for our kids is a struggle to answer this fundamental question, how do we decide who is right when people make competing claims about truth and reality? If someone says there is no God, everyone is free to do as they please, and someone says God exists and human behavior should conform to biblical principles, how do we decide who is right? If someone says gender is defined by biology, and someone says gender is fluid and biology has no influence, which perspective creates our laws? We can't have an ordered society without determining which statements are true and which views decide what is acceptable in society. To do this, people must determine what evidence and method of analysis they use to decide which perspective is correct. In our culture, the struggle is between logic and emotions, Judeo-Christianity and Marxism.

People have always struggled to agree on the evidence and perspectives they use to define the fundamental principles of society. Think about this for a moment: how do we define concepts of gender, private property, theft, murder, and even truth itself? What evidence, methods, and principles do we use to justify what we believe about truth and morality in our world? It's a question with a complex answer, and the methods and principles people rely on to answer these questions have never been fixed over time. New perspectives arise that lead to intellectual revolutions, creating new worldviews that compete for intellectual supremacy in a culture. It has happened throughout human history, and we are experiencing this battle in American culture today.

Traditional America and post-truth Marxism are fighting for intellectual supremacy in America right before our eyes. This battle is over the competing evidence, methods, and theories we use to define gender, racism, justice, sexuality, basic morality, and what's acceptable and just in our society. There's no other way to state this. You can't effectively help your kids if you don't understand this battle, and the road to understanding begins with a short trip through the history of ideas that brought these conflicting worldviews into existence. Our journey starts with the Enlightenment, the intellectual revolution that gave birth to America, and the traditional American worldview.

In the early seventeenth century, the philosopher René Descartes proposed a new method to understand truth and knowledge. He argued that logic and rational thought should guide the analysis of the world. Descartes proposed that all human beings could reach similar conclusions about reality if they relied on logic, critical thinking, and God-given self-evident facts and knowledge. Analyzing self-evident undeniable facts with logic gave conclusions that were established beyond doubt. This had tremendous potential for humanity. People had different opinions, but everyone had a rational mind. A shared logical analysis would provide similar conclusions about the nature of reality, thus dispelling people's many myths and opinions about how the world should be.[3, 4] This was a powerful intellectual tool, and, in many ways, Descartes was right—our modern world of technology, medicine, communication, and prosperity was built with this method. Here's how it works for a traditional American worldview.

Let's say we have a person named Aristotle and want to know if Aristotle is a man or woman. We could analyze facts with logic to answer the question. This might not seem very easy, but you use this method daily as you make your way through life. We would start with science to gain some facts and data about Aristotle. Observations tell us Aristotle has a Y chromosome and that everyone who has a Y chromosome is a man. We can analyze these

---

[3] *Encyclopedia Britannica Online*, "The rationalism of Descartes," last accessed December 27, 2022, https://www.britannica.com/topic/Western-philosophy/The-rationalism-of-Descartes.

[4] I chose Britannica as a source for its concise, accurate presentation of the main points of Descartes's rationalism, postmodern philosophy, and critical race theory. This is helpful for those who are encountering complex ideas for the first time. Technical works on these subjects can be overwhelming for those who are new to the basics of philosophy.

facts with logic to reach certain conclusions. It would work like this: Aristotle has a Y chromosome; all human beings who have a Y chromosome are men. Therefore, Aristotle is a man. Everyone who embraces a traditional American worldview uses this method to determine what is true about our world, providing an endless source of reliable information. It's the method of science and technology that transforms our lives. We have airplanes, space travel, clean water, health care, and cures for disease—the list is endless courtesy of the analysis of the world with logic and rational thought. Descartes's method became the intellectual foundation for Western civilization, the modern world, and America.

There are limitations to the knowledge this gives us. Facts and critical thinking can tell us that Aristotle is a man, but they don't tell us if Aristotle is a good man. We need another source of moral information to know if Aristotle is a good and acceptable member of society. Moral information helps us decide what is acceptable or unacceptable. Descartes and the intellectuals who birthed the Enlightenment were living in Christian Europe, and they turned to the principles of the Bible and the Judeo-Christian worldview for their moral content. They believed the God of the Bible gave self-evident, undoubtable, and objective (unchangeable) truth, providing moral information to build laws and acceptable behaviors in society.

Science and rational thought can tell us that Aristotle was a man, but Judeo-Christian principles gave moral information to evaluate whether Aristotle was a good man. If Aristotle was a good man, he wouldn't lie, steal, cheat on his wife, drink excessively, or participate in homosexual intimacy. He would treat people with kindness, love, patience, and respect for the concept of private property and the right of free individuals to determine their destiny as endowed by God. Most people are unaware that biblical principles had a profound influence, shaping every aspect of American society.

When people hear the word "Bible," they immediately react to the perceived "repressive" confines biblical morality places on the pursuit of pleasure and self-expression. Christianity's influence goes far beyond the limits to personal pleasure. We owe the entire structure of our society to the principles of the Judeo-Christian worldview, which has given us the following concepts that define the uniqueness of Western culture and traditional America: private property, English common law protecting individual rights, trial by jury, innocence until proven guilty, the sanctity of the body, sanctity of life, abolition of slavery, women's rights, right of self-determination, personal freedom, and liberty. There is far more to add, but each one is derived from biblical principles and unique to Western culture. The Enlightenment synthesis of Judeo-Christianity and rational thought created American society, its laws, and the traditional American worldview. Let me show you using an example from the Declaration of Independence. "We hold these truths to be self-evident, that all men are created equal, that they are endowed by their Creator with certain unalienable Rights, that among these are Life, Liberty, and the pursuit of Happiness."[5]

---

[5] "Declaration of Independence: A Transcription," National Archives, U.S. National Archives and Records Administration, 8 June 2022, https://www.archives.gov/founding-docs/declaration-transcript.

The principles that are the foundation of America are the product of the Enlightenment. "We hold these truths to be self-evident" identifies truth as self-evident, certain, beyond doubt, and clear to all who have a rational mind and use critical thinking. "That all men are created equal, that they are endowed by their Creator with certain unalienable Rights, that among these are Life, Liberty, and the pursuit of Happiness" declares God exists, created the universe, reveals the truth, and establishes certain undeniable self-evident rights for all human beings. This excerpt is a loosely formed logical argument. It demonstrates the Enlightenment at work in the minds of the Founding Fathers as they formed the principles that defined a radically new concept of government and society. Self-evident truth and rational thought guided by Judeo-Christian principles created the intellectual foundation that gave us America. Today, we rely on this worldview using facts, logic, and critical thinking guided by Judeo-Christian principles to order our world. Nearly half of our country uses a traditional American worldview to decide what is accurate and true and how we structure our society's laws and moral expectations.

The Enlightenment was a great intellectual revolution, and the modern world it created is unlike any other in history, but the assumptions Descartes made had flaws, and philosophers took advantage of them to challenge the intellectual credibility of his method. In their eyes, the Enlightenment was built on false assumptions and intellectual lies, which meant the entire method was corrupt. If the Enlightenment was corrupt, everything it produced was also corrupt, including America and the modern world. They claimed these societies were destructive and inherently oppressive, using reason, logic, science, and technology to destroy the environment and victimize other people.[6]

Postmodern philosophers claimed there were significant flaws within Descartes's assumptions about the existence of God and the undoubtable, self-evident nature of truth. Descartes's claims about the importance of using rational thought relied on God revealing self-evident, certain undoubtable truths, but truth is doubtable and not necessarily self-evident to those with different perspectives. Even facts weren't "certain"—they were open to interpretation. Science challenged God's existence, claiming the world could exist without Him. In the minds of the postmodern philosophers, God was an outdated myth and the story of Christianity was used to create a grand narrative that America was exceptional because it was built upon Christian principles. If God didn't exist, objective truth couldn't exist because He was the source. These challenges present serious implications for Descartes's method. If the assumptions were flawed, then the entire method Descartes proposed was corrupt. Postmodern philosophers rejected the entire foundation of the Enlightenment based on the flaws they perceived in Descartes's assumptions about self-evident, undoubtable knowledge.

If all their assumptions were valid, and the postmodern philosophers believed they were, it meant the fundamental assumptions of the Enlightenment were false, nothing but corrupt lies.

---

[6] *Encyclopedia Britannica Online*, Brian Duignan, "postmodernism," last modified December 23, 2022, https://www.britannica.com/topic/postmodernism-philosophy.

This meant logic, rational thought, and the puritanical nature of Judeo-Christian morality were myths, dishonest narratives used to build a corrupt society with social institutions that exploited the world. This is the postmodern movement; it argued that the Enlightenment and the modern world it created were corrupt because it was built upon a foundation of intellectual lies that used "facts," science, logic, and biblical principles to develop metanarratives, corrupt myths that justified patriarchy, slavery, xenophobia, the conquest of native lands, and the persecution of the LGBTQ community. America was not a nation of freedom and liberty but deeply marred by a history of exploitation and oppression resulting from the corrupt intellectual framework that created it.

Postmodernity became a philosophical wrecking ball that sought to intellectually attack and destroy the "corrupt" foundation of Enlightenment knowledge and the "corrupt" societies it created. The movement attempts to deconstruct every aspect of the modern world and America, and it's undeniably succeeded in creating a pile of intellectual rubble from the Enlightenment framework for knowledge and morality. But its success created a profound problem for humanity; postmodernity destroyed the philosophical framework for the modern world without providing a new framework in its place. This is critical because human beings need a paradigm for understanding knowledge and morality. Even though people deny truth and morality exist, a society can't function without a paradigm to understand what is real and morally acceptable.

People say there is no such thing as truth and morality; you have your truth, they have their truth, and there is no inherent right or wrong. That may be the world they want, but it's not the world they want to live in. Go to their house and tell them that there is no right or wrong, then take their stuff. I guarantee they will demand you obey laws based on a moral paradigm. They'll paraphrase Genesis by saying some form of, "Thou shall not steal." People need a moral structure to order society; they can't live in chaos. If they don't have one, they'll create one, which is precisely what's happening today. As people crawled from the intellectual rubble of the postmodern movement, they created a new intellectual paradigm, the post-truth Marxist worldview, out of necessity. The post-truth Marxist worldview fills the intellectual void created by the postmodern attack on the Enlightenment. It's the new moral paradigm of the Left and your child's public education. That's why it's critical for you to understand what it is and how it influences your kids.

Let's start with what it means to be post-truth.

In 2016, the prestigious Oxford dictionary chose post-truth as its "Word of the Year," which best describes the intellectual mood of the Western world. Here's how they defined it.

> "Post-truth is the condition relating to or defining circumstances in which objective facts are less influential in shaping public opinion than appeals to emotion and personal belief."[7]

---

[7] Joshua Norman, "'Post-truth' named word of the year for 2016 by Oxford Dictionaries," CBS News, November 17, 2016, https://www.cbsnews.com/news/post-truth-word-of-the-year-2016-oxford-dictionaries/.

YOU SPEAK FACTS; THEY SPEAK EMOJI

People put feelings above facts when they evaluate the world, relying on emotions rather than logic and rational thought. This means that what they feel dictates reality; they order their world based on what conforms to their feelings and emotions. Post-truth has replaced critical thinking for a growing segment of our country and your kids. Here's how this works. Let's return to our example about Aristotle to demonstrate how post-truth operates in our world. Aristotle has a Y chromosome; Aristotle **FEELS** like a woman. Therefore, Aristotle is a woman.

Post-truth is now substituted for logic and critical thought. A growing segment of our population defines reality as that which conforms to feelings and emotions rather than the rational analysis of facts and data. This is precisely why gender is fluid in the mind of the Progressive Left—it's defined by feeling, not biology, and they work to ensure your children adopt this post-truth approach to "knowledge," replacing the use of logic with emotions in every area of life. As we will see in later chapters, it's a significant influence behind the creation of the social justice narratives like the LGBTQ movement and critical race theory, and its power is only growing. This is the reason the conservative editor emeritus of the Daily Wire, Ben Shapiro, challenges woke college students during debates with his infamous, "Facts don't care about your feelings."[8] It's a direct response to post-truth's influence on the intellectual development of today's college students. Your kids are given

---

[8] Ben Shapiro, *Facts Don't Care About Your Feelings* (Hermosa Beach: Creators Publishing, 2019).

post-truth interpretations of the world in school, and it's becoming their method to determine what constitutes "reality."

Let's continue. For the moment, we'll accept post-truth assumptions.

The fact that Aristotle "is" a woman because Aristotle feels like a woman is only half of our equation. Post-truth cannot tell us whether Aristotle is a good "woman." The survivors of postmodernism's destruction of the Enlightenment needed a new source of moral information once it rejected the Judeo-Christian worldview. It chose Marxism.

Marxism has been adapted to the American cultural story and has become the moral paradigm for the post-truth Marxist worldview. Two essential aspects of the current form of Marxism manifesting in this worldview influence your children. The first is social conditioning. In the nineteenth and twentieth centuries, social theorists proposed the concept that society was a distinct entity that had the primary influence in creating the identities of people. Social institutions set the norms that shaped the ideas and behaviors of any individual. This meant that society had the primary influence and control over the identities and actions of the people living within them. In his writings, Karl Marx proposed that societies create social relationships, even the thoughts of human beings. Over time, this concept has been developed, becoming the dominant view of the Progressive Left. From their perspective, societies and their institutions shape everything about us—race, gender, and sexuality, and every identity people adopt results from the influence of social institutions, not biology or an inherent individual personality. The social structures of society create the roles and personas that people assume in life. The Progressive Left claims that an oppressive patriarchy creates traditional women's gender roles that result from men demanding women adopt a traditional position to facilitate their success in society.[9, 10, 11, 12]

Social institutions that cause oppression and exploitation profoundly influence everything about our society, shaping all the choices people make about their behavior. People steal, not because of personal moral failure but because economic exploitation creates inequalities, rich versus poor, that force the poor to steal to survive. Thieves aren't thieves; they're victims reacting to their environment. This concept of social conditioning dominates the Progressive view of how society functions. From their perspective, society creates every aspect of the person—gender, race, and ethnicity, and every aspect of human beings is socially conditioned. They are made by society and can be whatever a community agrees they should be. In

---

[9] "Gender," Psychology Today, last accessed December 29, 2022, https://www.psychologytoday.com/us/basics/gender.

[10] This Psychology Today article provides an excellent example of the current understanding of gender as a product of social conditioning. Social conditioning is the defining force that shapes all aspects of human identity including race and sexuality in the mind of the Progressive Left.

[11] *Encyclopedia Britannica Online* "Basic tenets of critical race theory," accessed January 10, 2023, https://www.britannica.com/topic/critical-race-theory/Basic-tenets-of-critical-race-theory

[12] Like all aspects of humanity, Race is socially conditioned in the mind of the Progressive Left. Take a moment to read the Britannica summary of critical race theory which begins with the declaration that race is socially constructed and is not the product of inherited physical or behavioral differences.

a post-truth Marxist worldview, social experiences create concepts of sexual identity, lifestyle, and gender. That's why gender has no basis in biology for the Progressive Left. Gender can be whatever society and people feel it should be.

The second significant influence is that morality and justice are a product of how society constructs its social institutions. Institutions condition behavior and control positive or negative outcomes for everyone. Societies are responsible for everything that happens because of how their institutions are designed and influence people. Social institutions designed to create and facilitate exploitation, oppression, and victimization, like slavery, patriarchy, and capitalism, incite people to commit slavery, patriarchy, and economic exploitation. The systems bear the responsibility for a person's behavior. People are simply victims of a society's structure, influenced to behave by the exploitation and victimization that are built into its institutions.

This introduces a new concept of justice, social justice, which places the ultimate responsibility for a just society in the design of social institutions, not on the demands of individual character. Social justice seeks to create a society with institutions designed to achieve fairness, tolerance, and equity (equality of outcome). This requires that the corrupt institutions of traditional America, which were built upon the exploitation and victimization from the failed assumptions of the Enlightenment, must be torn down and a new society constructed on the principles of social justice be built in its place. In theory, humanity can end suffering through social engineering when they replace oppressive institutions with those that achieve equality, fairness, and equal outcomes for everyone. LGBTQ, critical race theory, and cancel culture apply social justice concepts to achieve fairness and equity for every race and lifestyle. The pursuit of social justice becomes the moral framework of the post-truth Marxist worldview.

This is the post-truth Marxist worldview: people order "reality" based on their feelings and define moral virtue as the pursuit of social justice, deconstructing the corrupt social institutions of traditional America and building a new society that achieves equity.

The post-truth Marxist world sees this in absolute terms. They want to end the continual suffering traditional America brings to the world because racism, patriarchy, sexism, homophobia, transphobia, xenophobia, and income inequality are built into every one of its institutions. American society must be deconstructed and rebuilt to social justice standards, achieving equity at all costs. This makes the reeducation of children an absolute necessity. From the Progressive perspective, traditional America has spent more than two centuries perpetuating Enlightenment myths of American exceptionalism, justifying slavery, racism, homophobia, transphobia, patriarchy, and the economic exploitation of capitalism. The lies of the Enlightenment and its Judeo-Christian influence must be undone, and it starts by reeducating kids in public schools.

That's why indoctrinating kids to accept a post-truth Marxist worldview at the earliest ages is a critical part of the transformation of American society. Kindergarten Drag Queen Story Hour has a purpose. It's a complete expression of the worldview, teaching five-year-olds that socially conditioned sexuality has no boundaries.

White teens are taught that they're privileged young white supremacists who cannot see the structural racism they protect and promote. Cancel culture is ready to cast out kids who don't conform, handing out substantial social punishments for kids who don't follow complete obedience. There's a method to the madness, and it's exceptionally effective when it's introduced as sacrosanct truth to the young impressionable minds of kids who don't have the freedom to learn or present counter perspectives.

When kids embrace this post-truth Marxist worldview, they adopt an antithetical and openly hostile perspective to traditional America. That's why it's so difficult to have conversations that reason with them. We are speaking two different moral languages; we hold onto a traditional American worldview, and as post-truth Marxists, they are taught to despise everything about America. They react with feelings and anger if we try to reason with them using data and logic. We speak facts; they speak emoji, and you'll have to learn an entirely new approach to protect them.

The following chapters have the information and strategies you need to effectively challenge indoctrination and protect your kids using the insights and information that I'll provide. LGBTQ ideals, critical race theory, and cancel culture develop from the perspectives I've just shared. They are a product of intellectual development that has been transforming American society for over a century. I'll explain how they were constructed and equip you to protect kids effectively. But everything depends on the information in this chapter; the keys to protecting your children are found in the ideas we've just covered. I recommend you reread this chapter a couple of times. Your ability to challenge social justice narratives will depend on how well you understand these two worldviews and how they operate. Understanding each will help you engage the detailed arguments as we progress.

First, we need to talk about the essential part of this journey that you must embrace if you're going to protect your kids.

CHAPTER 3

The Time You Spend Together Makes the Difference

Your relationship with your kids is your most important resource to protect them. I want to think it's the information I'm providing, but I can tell you from experience that protecting them will be difficult if you can't have meaningful conversations with them. Here's why. It's almost impossible to reason with kids who live a post-truth reality and invest emotionally in the Marxist victimization narratives. How can you reason with someone who feels that transgender students experience the violence of hate and intolerance because people refuse to accept that gender is fluid and defined by feelings? Confronting post-truth with logic leads to conflict every time. Challenging social justice narratives requires you to take a journey with your kids, engaging them in conversations that get them to think critically about the ideas they are being indoctrinated with. This involves asking questions that expose the deep-seated intellectual flaws of these ideologies and the unfortunate realities they create when they impact their own lives.

Conversations that ask questions are CRITICAL when you challenge LGBTQ and critical race theory because questions expose the failures of these positions in ways kids can accept and understand. These ideologies intimidate parents because they are presented as unassailable sacrosanct truth, but don't let anyone fool you—they have deep-seated, fatal intellectual flaws that even your kids can see once exposed. Questions do the work for you because they challenge your kids to think beyond the woke assumptions they have been given as sacrosanct truth. People often make an argument based on a premise, a narrow set of assumptions that work for a limited set of circumstances. If you accept the assumptions, you allow them to define the boundaries of a conversation. Once you accept the premise, it's almost impossible to challenge. You must expose the flaws of the premise with questions if you're going to be successful. When you expose the weaknesses of an argument, people are forced to come to terms with the intellectual failures of their position. It sounds complicated, but once you see it work, it's easy to understand and apply.

Here's an example:

"When did you stop beating your (wife, dog, child, etc.)?" It's the classic example of a loaded question because it's built on a premise of controversial and flawed assumptions presented as though they are known to be accurate, that is, you're a proven abuser. It's infuriating and makes us immediately defensive because the question "convicts" us of something we've never done without offering proof. Understanding how to engage these arguments is essential because you'll hear an endless supply of these when you're talking to your kids about social justice. Be prepared for, "Why do you hate the trans community?" or "Why can't you see systemic racism and your white privilege?" The question "Why do you hate the trans community?" assumes the premise that you hating the trans community is true and sets that as the starting point for conversation. Your response is critical. If you're not careful, you'll react, trying to defend yourself with a conversation that attempts to prove you don't hate the trans community. Once you've gone that route, you've lost the argument and started a heated exchange that leads nowhere. Challenging the assumptions of the accusation with questions is the only way to win these debates. Here's how it works.

Let's start with, "When did you stop beating your dog?" You've already lost the argument if you defend yourself against the accusation. If you respond with an indignant, "I've never beaten my dog," you'll spend the rest of the conversation defending yourself against something you've never done. Once you've acknowledged that the premise that you're someone who beats their dog is an idea that must be defended, you're allowing that to define the following discussion. It's nearly impossible to win once you've allowed a false premise to define an argument. Instead, you challenge the premise with questions, demonstrating the intellectual failures of the idea.

The way to respond is by asking a question that challenges the premise's false assumptions and reveals the argument's motive. Here's the reply: "Your question has no basis in factual reality. Why do you want to slander me and destroy my reputation by asking a question that implies I'm a reprehensible human being?" The response redirects the argument from the implication that you're a despicable human being to the reality at hand. The questioner wants to slander you by asking a leading question with no basis. This shifts the focus of the loaded question from the accusation that you beat your dog to the actual premise of the argument, which is the intent to slander you by implying that you're a violent and unacceptable human being.

When you challenge the false premise of the accusation, you reframe the argument in a way that reveals what's happening; you expose the slander, forcing the questioner to acknowledge what they've done. Once the duplicity is out in the open, it moves the argument into a new arena that puts you in a position to succeed. Remember, it's almost impossible to disprove the charge that you beat your dog because it's difficult to prove that something never happened. But once the lies and slander are out in the open, you've exposed the real agenda, making this the topic moving forward.

Be prepared; when you talk with your kids about social justice, you will get a long list of loaded questions and statements. You can only prevail by asking questions in conversations that expose the failed assumptions of the arguments. The narratives about critical race theory and the LGBTQ agenda are built on an endless series of false assumptions presented as sacrosanct truth. They are easily exposed once questioned, but you must be ready. Your kids will bring a long list of emotionally based accusations in the form of loaded statements and questions when you push back. If you're not careful, you'll be defending yourself against an endless list of accusations that have no basis in reality. Here's what this looks like.

If you refuse to accept the trans community and LGBTQ agenda without question, you'll be labeled an intolerant hater and transphobe. They'll ask, "Why are you such a hater? Why do you hate the trans community?" It's a loaded question. If you try to defend yourself against the accusation that you hate the trans community, it's the same as trying to disprove the allegation that you're a violent and reprehensible human being. You'll be responding to an argument built on false assumptions, transforming the conversation into a heated one that leads nowhere. You must respond with a different strategy that challenges the false assumptions of social justice narratives. To succeed, you'll need informed strategies, which I'll provide in the coming chapters, and a relationship with your kids that leads to great conversations.

Your relationship with your kids is the most significant factor determining your ability to protect them from the indoctrination they receive in their public schools because your relationship is about communication and trust. It's hard to succeed without these. Communication is vital because challenging social justice narratives is a process that takes time; it's not a matter of "winning" with a single knockout logical argument. Remember back to the chapter *You Speak Facts; They Speak Emoji*—your kids are using their feelings to dictate reality. If they feel you're a hater because they bought into an emotionally driven narrative that anything less than complete tolerance of the trans community is transphobic hatred, in that case, you'll never argue them out of the position using logic. It takes conversations where you can ask legitimate questions that challenge the fundamental assumptions behind the LGBTQ agenda and the Left's assertion that disagreement equals hate.

These conversations are incredibly effective when they happen over time, so don't go for the immediate knockout win. Kids must process information to deal with the challenges and reach conclusions. Once they understand the failures of social justice narratives, they can recognize the failures of the ideologies and their impact on their communities and personal lives. This is a journey you must take with them, and most of all, they must trust you because rejecting woke narratives will thoroughly shake up their world. Earning their trust is critical.

Social justice narratives represent far more than philosophical ideologies for kids in school; they represent their social relationships and identities. Kids who refuse to embrace woke culture get canceled and cast out of social circles, which devastates them. Educators and administrators ensure that social justice narratives and the post-truth Marxist worldview are the reigning paradigms for public education; alternative positions are rarely accepted in classrooms. Kids don't have the option of considering different worldviews, and as each year passes, more kids get the indoctrination, making it the reigning orthodoxy of schools and social circles. Those who refuse to accept woke culture face cancel culture, which hands out tremendous social punishment to anyone who refuses to walk in lockstep to social justice narratives. It's conform or be cast out, and getting cast out of social circles is emotional suicide for kids who define their identity and self-worth through social relationships.

It's critical for parents to recognize that challenging social justice narratives amounts to challenging their child's social identities, which is the entire world of teenagers. This seems like a simple intellectual process for parents to choose the correct interpretation of reality. But kids face cancel culture and the complete disintegration of their worlds when they reject the narratives. It's an arduous journey, and they must trust your relationship's strength every step of the way to make it. Your relationship with your kids is more important than you realize; it's more important than the information you bring. I want you to understand that every day you pursue a relationship with your child, you build a hedge of protection around them. Here's your homework. After you're done with this chapter, set aside time to do something with your child to accomplish two critical goals: develop conversation and build trust.

Learn how to talk with your kids before you have conversations with them about social justice. Have conversations with them about the things they like, even if you don't like the topic, and listen more than you speak. You want to make communication with them comfortable and natural. Conversations about social justice are complex, and difficult conversations aren't the time to learn how to talk with them. Difficult conversations are more effortless with people you know how to communicate effectively, so start talking with your kids today. If you have teens, they're challenging human beings; I get it. Talking with them is like prying secrets from the CIA. That's why you need to set time aside to do things with them because activities build trust and time for conversation.

When you set time aside to do things with your kids, they understand that you're taking a genuine interest in them, especially when you are doing something they want to do. Let them decide on a favorite activity and do it without question (I GUARANTEE they will talk then). You build a bond of trust with them when you do things they enjoy. This is the trust they will need when you begin challenging woke narratives. I have the best conversations with my sons when we are outside doing simple things like stacking firewood. My youngest devolves into a verbal neanderthal when I pick him up after school; he's tired and I get grunt responses to every question. I still ask him how his day went, but I have to interpret answers that are little more than a single word. At this point, I've pretty much given up on two-way conversations in the afternoons. Things change when we spend other time together, and the conversation is nonstop during a trip to the rifle range, deer hunting, or building projects. I'm always dragging my boys out of the house to do things together.

Spending time builds relationships; it's the key to unlocking their minds. Your children want and need time with you. Every minute you spend connecting with them paves the way for effective communication and trust. It's the special sauce that makes the challenging conversations work. But you have to start TODAY. Find out what they want to do, then set aside the time to change their world together.

I want you to put the book down and look at your schedule. Don't read any further until you've had a conversation and have scheduled time to spend with each of your kids. Don't try to find time; MAKE time. Remember, it's not a one-time event but the beginning of a new way of relating to them that can transform their lives.

Have you scheduled time and finished your homework? Now it's time to equip you with the information and strategies you need to change their world.

CHAPTER 4

Kindergarten Drag Queen Story Hour

There's no better demonstration of the post-truth Marxist worldview at work in culture than the LGBTQ agenda. It combines the best of everything: emotionally defined reality, socially conditioned sexuality, and an endless list of oppression/victimization narratives because traditional America refuses to embrace Kindergarten Drag Queen Story Hour and Minor Attracted Persons (pedophiles). The twilight zone becomes a reality, "Imagine, if you will, an America where parents end up on a domestic terror watch list because they refuse to normalize drag queens and pedophilia." Orwell warned us in *1984* that the unimaginable was possible. [13]

In the post-truth Marxist world, emotions and social conditioning define gender and sexuality. It's a complete and radical departure from traditional America's view, and it sends parents reeling from the implications, wondering how they fight these narratives. Most parents charge ahead with straightforward arguments quoting Bible verses and presenting their opinions

---

[13] George Orwell, *1984* (New York: Signet Classics, 1977).

and objections. These are important to us as parents, but more and more kids refuse to give them any value. They dismiss them as having any authority over the discussion. I found that asking the proper series of questions shattered the foundations of the LGBTQ agenda, opening the door for many conversations that mattered to me as a parent.

The approach I'm sharing challenges the assumptions of the LGBTQ agenda using a specific series of questions that work best when you follow the format. I'll demonstrate how this works and how it was successful for me in my world. First, we must understand how the LGBTQ agenda develops and functions in culture. Once you see, you'll understand how protecting your children becomes evident.

We start with the post-truth's use of emotional content to determine what defines gender and socially acceptable sexuality.

Emotions and preferences, how someone FEELS about gender and sexuality, become the criteria that define gender and sexuality. Let's return to the discussion about post-truth from the chapter *You Speak Facts; They Speak Emoji*. In a post-truth world, emotions dictate reality. The fact that Aristotle has a Y chromosome does not influence Aristotle's gender. Aristotle defines gender based on his feelings and preferences. In a post-truth Marxist world, Aristotle is a woman because he feels like a woman. The fact that he has a Y chromosome has zero influence.

When people are asked why they choose a particular gender or gender-fluid status, they respond from a position of preferred emotional experiences. They feel more positive, empowered, and affirmed, have less anxiety, and feel free from being trapped in a body that doesn't conform to their feelings; emotional content defines gender. This means gender can be defined in any manner that conforms to the subjective nature of emotions, shattering the traditional binary, either male or female, categorization. A person's gender can shift between male, female, or a hybrid combination of the two at any given moment in response to their changing preferences, which do not have to manifest in any change in outward appearance.

In the past, members of the transgender community often tracked their gender by changing their appearance to conform to a biologically based concept of male or female or choosing gender reassignment surgery. Not today, when post-truth emotions dictate "reality." A person can identify as any concept of gender without any changes to their appearance, making it impossible for anyone to know or predict where they are on the gender spectrum at any given moment. This has led to the development of preferred pronouns and the emerging legislation that demands the rest of the world use them.

Personal pronouns are novel words that reflect a person's understanding of their inclusion on the gender spectrum. They are designed to reflect the convoluted world of gender when the complex nature of human emotions characterizes it. Post-truth concepts of gender can be an integration of male and female or shifts between them conforming to the changing nature of human perceptions and desires. People can identify as female in the morning, male at work, and female once they return home. The pronouns were invented to communicate this complex "reality." The LGBTQ agenda demands that everyone universally use a transgender person's pronouns when addressing them. Calling someone by their incorrect pronoun is called misgendering, and it's considered an act of oppression, victimization, and violence.

Here are the startling facts behind LGBTQ's demands for radically overturning the entire social architecture of gender in America. The Williams Institute, a division of UCLA's law school that exists for LGBTQ protections, estimates there are currently 1.6 million members of the transgender community in America.[14] Using current US census figures, that amounts to 0.5 percent of the current population. It's critical to understand that the post-truth Marxist world wants to completely shatter the social architecture of gender to accommodate the emotional preferences of 0.5 percent of the population. Dwell on that for a moment.

If you come from a traditional American mindset, you're asking yourself, how did we get here? Since when did one person's emotional content give them the right to redefine gender and completely reconstruct the social order of America? Welcome to the marriage of post-truth and the development of social conditioning.[15]

The Progressive Left proposes that all the characteristics of a person—their race, gender, sexual identity and preference, and

---

[14] "How Many Adults and Youth Identify as Transgender in the United States," UCLA School of Law – Williams Institute, accessed December 26, 2022, https://williamsinstitute.law.ucla.edu/publications/trans-adults-united-states/.

[15] "Gender," Psychology Today, accessed December 29, 2022, https://www.psychologytoday.com/us/basics/gender.

relationships—are all socially constructed, the product of the influence of their society. Traditional gender roles for boys and girls are constructs of traditional American society, forcing biblically influenced patriarchal gender roles on children from infancy. Boys don't necessarily like trucks, and girls don't love pink because their chromosomes confer biological distinctions that predispose them. Boys like trucks and girls wear pink because generations of parents continue to perpetuate gender stereotypes from birth. Fathers give boys trucks for their first birthday, and mothers dress their girls in pink because that's how it's always been and always should be; parents define gender from prejudice.

The post-truth Marxist world sees traditional gender roles as patriarchal stereotypes born from the prejudicial myths of Enlightenment biblical narratives. These stereotypes are forms of oppression that have forced generations to deny their true gender identities by shaming them into adopting traditional gender roles. Post-truth Marxists refuse to accept traditional definitions and limits on gender. Gender has no distinctions in a world that has no God. How can there be fundamental inherent differences between the sexes if there is no God to create them? If God doesn't exist, society, and its conditioning are all that humanity has, and the oppression caused by prejudicial stereotypes must end.

This is the precise reasoning they use to justify their deconstruction of the social architecture of gender in America based on the emotional preferences of 0.5 percent of the population. It's almost incomprehensible, but this is what the post-truth Marxist deconstruction of society and implementation of social justice looks like when they apply their theory to end oppression and achieve equity. That's why the fight for public policy that sets boundaries to protect the majority view of the 99.5 percent of Americans who are comfortable with their gender that conforms to biology needs to happen immediately. The narrative needs to focus on protecting the rights of the 99.5 percent who had no interest in giving men unfettered access to women's protected spaces and sports before the rise of the LGBTQ agenda. No one wants to see the transgender community ridiculed or persecuted. Still, the gender architecture of society should conform to the orientation of the 99.5 percent who are comfortable with the gender of their birth, which means biology, regardless of the emotional preferences and perceptions of 0.5 percent of the population. This should be a primary point carried forward as parents and legislators push back in society. With each incremental victory, Progressives set striking precedents in the battle for public policy, which has far reaching implications. This worldview has few limits on gender, sexual identity, and practice, and they want to normalize every perspective in America.

In a post-truth Marxist world, gender, sexual identity, and sexual preference are ideas conditioned and affirmed by society, which means gender can be ANYTHING anyone feels, and society approves. There should be no restrictions on gender whatsoever, especially myths of Judeo-Christian concepts of men and women created by God with inherent differences expressed because of their biology. The same holds for sexuality. Every sexual preference is acceptable. Sexuality becomes whatever people desire, and society affirms. And society is ready to affirm anything. Judeo-Christian views limiting acceptable forms of sexuality to those practiced within heterosexual marriage are the quintessential example of the oppressive, intolerant, homophobic, and transphobic hatred originating from a failed Enlightenment biblical worldview.

Progressives seek to exile any hint of Judeo-Christian morality from culture, refusing to accept any restrictions or limitations on expressions of gender or sexuality. But the push for ultimate freedom and acceptance of the ever-expanding gender and sexuality community came with some foreseen consequences. I'll explain. Initially, this identity group identified as lesbian, gay, then bisexual (LGB), but the push for the acceptance of the expansion of sexual expression led to the demand that any remaining social barriers be removed. Identity groups were expanding gender and sexuality, demanding unqualified acceptance, which meant the affirmation and acceptance of any personal choice. That's why there is an expansion of letters within the LGBTQ lexicon. Each new sub-community's expression receives a letter designation, and LGB expands to LGBTQ+ and beyond.

Conservatives responded that eventually, there would be no boundaries, no barriers, and everything would be acceptable under the infinite umbrella of tolerance. The response from the Left was, "How dare you imply that people would eventually want to marry an animal, a robot with the capacity for sexual intimacy, or the demand that the MAPs—Minor attracted persons (people who legitimize sexual intimacy with children)—be granted legitimacy. But that's precisely where we are. If everything is socially conditioned, everyone is forced to embrace whatever form of sexuality society affirms. This is precisely the MAP community's argument in its fight for normalization.

Conservatives were right. The "furries" emerged once Pandora's box opened, demanding litter boxes and legitimacy. Furries believe they are other forms of life trapped in a human body and are often referred to as the otherkin.[16] You have Worm Kin, Cat Kin, Dog Kin, Fairy Kin, and Tree Kin. People demand to be recognized as another form of life: cat, dog, fairy, worm, tree, fern—the list is endless. They believe they exist as other forms of life trapped in human bodies, demanding the world affirm their positions because of their feelings, preferences, and desires. Once Pandora's box of post-truth social conditioning opens, there is no end to the machinations of human emotions. People will demand legitimacy for every desire.

The post-truth Marxist Left demands infinite tolerance of every culturally affirmed position on gender identity and sexual orientation; anything less is considered an act of oppression, victimization, and violence inflicted on the LGBTQ community. Your children are indoctrinated to accept this as a concrete reality. They won't have a class that teaches them to reject logic. They are conditioned to reject traditional American views of gender and sexuality as failed relics of an antiquated morality and affirm every gender

---

[16] Joseph p. Laycock, "We Are Spirits of Another Sort," Ontological Rebellion and Religious Dimensions of the Otherkin Community, Novo Religio: The Journal of Alternate and Emergent Religions Vol 15, no. 3 (February 2012) pp. 65-90, https://www.jstor.org/stable/10.1525/nr.2012.15.3.65.

and sexual expression with complete tolerance. Kids are taught to accept every lifestyle; intolerance equals hate and violence.

Their indoctrination begins as early as preschool to minimize the influence of the traditional American worldview and your influence at home. This is precisely why parents are concerned about the fight for their children. As the Progressive Left gains greater control over schools, it allows them to establish a post-truth Marxist perspective of socially conditioned gender and sexual identity for your kids at the earliest ages. This is precisely why Kindergarten Drag Queen Story Hour is necessary from a post-truth Marxist point of view. It's the ultimate attempt to normalize post-truth sexuality at the earliest ages. It teaches kids that everything is a fair game within socially conditioned gender and sexual preferences. Recognize this: your school administrators and teachers want your kids to recognize drag queens and furries as appropriate forms of human expression. As this trajectory continues, the MAPs aren't far behind.

I realize that's a lot of information, but you'll need it when you have conversations with your kids. All of this comes into play as you challenge the agenda, which is where we're shifting. You have the philosophical basis for the indoctrination and how it's playing out. The question is, what do you do now that you have the information and you've reached the point of talking with your kids?

I'll start with what you shouldn't do. Don't try to present logical arguments to them. Remember, logic has been discredited, and they like relying on their emotions. All they'll do is react with anger. You won't get anywhere; you'll drive them further into woke culture. Also, you must be careful with arguments from authority. I'll explain and I need you to carefully consider what I'm saying.

Parents often begin challenging the LGBTQ agenda with arguments using the history of America, their personal feelings, or biblical passages as authoritative information to win a position. These are arguments from "authorities," and they're often only effective when everyone agrees on the truth behind the authority. If your kids don't respect the source you cite, they'll reject any argument based on it. Remember that your kids have spent years listening to narratives that have destroyed the credibility of traditional America and the influence of biblical Christianity. Consider the latest evidence that shows that two-thirds of teens from conservative churches leave their walk with God when they leave home. Woke culture is eroding the faith of our children.

The latest Barna surveys show that most teens in conservative churches have little knowledge of or confidence in Christianity and biblical principles. This means most kids don't have the same confidence in their faith as their parents do. They feel contemporary Christianity can't provide effective answers to the challenges of our current culture.[17] If the Bible is your only go-to argument, you might find it has little influence if your kids don't respect it. That's the reality of the world we live in. I'm not saying that biblical principles or your perspectives have no influence here; they do. Each line of evidence we use has its place and purpose. It's essential to

---

[17] "Six Reasons Young Christians Leave the Church," Barna Group, September 27, 2011, https://www.barna.com/research/six-reasons-young-christians-leave-church/.

understand how they all work together, using them at the appropriate times. There are many different avenues we take to challenge this indoctrination. Here's what I found to be the most effective starting point in this journey.

To be effective here, you must challenge the failures and limitations of the fundamental assumptions that are the basis of the LGBTQ ideology and the way it works within the culture. You'll accomplish this by having an ongoing conversation with your children, asking a series of directed questions. Asking legitimate questions is one of the essential tools in debate or apologetics. Here's why: questions expose limitations that cause your kids to think about the failed assumptions LGBTQ ideology is based on.

Here's the strategy.

First, ask them questions that define the primary ideological position in a way that everyone can agree upon. You're establishing how LGBTQ ideology works in a way they can understand. Then ask a series of follow-up questions that moves their ideological position outside of LGBTQ's protected assumptions, demonstrating its failures. Here's how this works, and here's how it worked for me.

After nearly losing my mind hearing the defense of the transgender ideology and the accusation that I was a hateful transphobe because I didn't want to accept the transgender agenda, I chose to ask some questions. I started by asking why an individual with a Y chromosome can be considered a woman in a gender-fluid world. It took a few minutes until we all agreed that it was based upon a person's feelings; a person felt better and more like a woman than a man. I said, "Okay, I'll accept that gender has no basis in biology.

It's all about the feelings and preferences that a society affirms." I said, "Cool, let's go with that. Do we agree?" And they said yes. These questions defined the LGBTQ ideological position, and we all agreed. The follow-up questions caused them to shift.

I looked at them and said, "What if I felt like I was Black? Since gender wasn't tied to biology, race shouldn't be tied to biology. What's to stop me from identifying as Black?" The response was predictable. "No way, you're White; you can't do that." I looked at them and said, "If it's okay for someone with a Y chromosome to identify as a woman when they're biologically not a woman, then there's nothing wrong with me identifying as being Black, even though I have no Black genetics. If it's all about feelings, then it should work." You can predict the response. I pushed it one step further because if everything is socially conditioned, everything is socially conditioned. If feelings dictate reality, then the following should apply.

I said, "Now I'm identifying as female, so you need to acknowledge me as a Black woman." And the emotional content of the response amped up. I pushed it further and said, "You know, I'm over fifty, and I've done a lot of physical work in my life. There are times I wake up with aches and pains, and based on the level of pain I feel in my body, I identify as disabled. Since I'm a woman and am attracted to women, I identify as a lesbian. So, I have a question for you, can you give me any reason why I shouldn't update my resume to identify as a disabled, Black lesbian to compete within the corporate world looking for affirmative action preferences?"

My oldest son was horrified and was old enough to recognize that possibility's impact. He said, "You can't do that." I said, "Yes, I can because if everything is socially conditioned based upon feelings and preferences, then anything is fair game." He wanted to dismiss that argument and move on to something else, but I refused to let him do that. I said to him, "Look, we're not going to have any more conversation about this until you can give me a valid reason why it's okay for someone with a Y chromosome to identify as a woman, but it's not okay for me to identify as a disabled, Black lesbian. I'm only using LGBTQ's own rules."

The conversation ended, and I let it sit for a while. There were times when other things would come up in conversation that were parallel, but I would say, "You know, I love you. But I can't move forward in this conversation until you're willing to tell me why it's not okay for me, as a non-disabled, heterosexual, White male to identify as a disabled, Black lesbian. I'm only using the rules we agreed upon from the LGBTQ community. I'd like you to tell me why one is okay but the other isn't." It takes time, but the strategy works.

You can take this further by questioning how the LGBTQ ideology personally impacts your kids or their friends within the world they live in. You can do this with the impact of biological males identifying as transwomen and crushing girls' high school and collegiate athletics. Start by asking your kids a question that sets the parameters you will use when you propose a different scenario. It would work like this.

Ask them, "Do I correctly understand that in the past, patriarchy was defined as someone with a Y chromosome dominating and excluding women from succeeding in society? Then why isn't it a form of patriarchal oppression when an individual with a Y chromosome is crushing women's high school athletics because they have an unfair biological advantage? How is that not a new form of oppressive patriarchy? Why is it so important that the feelings of trans athletes override the feelings of an entire group of young women who have been working incredibly hard for their entire lives? How is this new form of patriarchy acceptable?"

It's essential to capitalize on questions about the furries. Ask them if they are truly prepared to deal with people who demand to be accepted as animals or fairies. Will they fully accept people as cats based on their emotional preferences? Do we put a litter box in your classroom? Do we have litter boxes in bathrooms? If you had a child that came home and said he was a frog, are you willing to raise him as a frog? Ask them if this ever ends and if they are prepared to live in the world this creates. Politely remind them that you would like a legitimate answer.

Be prepared for the reactions you're going to get, but calmly remind them that this is the world they will live in. The rules of the agenda make everything fair game, and that's the world they are creating for themselves. As you can see, the LGBTQ ideology works under a very narrow set of protected assumptions and utterly fails when the principles are forced to operate outside its protected circumstances. Post-truth social conditioning works when limited to a narrowly defined set of personal expressions. Take every opportunity to push it beyond the protected space.

It is essential to remember these two points. First, be patient, and let these questions speak over time; the battle is not won overnight. Second, you're going to get reactions; don't react to them. Keep calmly returning them to the questions and ask for answers. If they can't answer or choose not to give you an answer, move on to a subject other than social justice concerns. But the next time they want to talk about some aspect of social justice, politely remind them you're still looking for an answer to your question. Don't let the conversations switch to different topics if they attempt to avoid answering, or at least politely let them know they are refusing to answer and you expect one at another time.

Using questions opened the door to broader conversations for my kids and me. I posed legitimate concerns that I wanted to talk about, and I wanted to know what they thought. Did they feel it was fair for me to identify as a disabled, Black lesbian to gain a competitive advantage for hiring when I'm not a disabled, Black lesbian? If my feelings can't make me a disabled, Black lesbian, how are we expected to declare someone a cat based on their emotional preferences? I wanted to know how they would react to someone who said they were a cat and demanded they agree to that "reality."

It's critical to present this as a legitimate conversation, not an agenda. If they feel you're attempting to gain intellectual victory, it won't work. The questions are designed to make them honestly consider the failure of the LGBTQ assumptions because they are the only ones who can change their minds and reject the indoctrination. Once kids recognize the implications and challenges of emotionally affirmed social conditioning, they begin to let their guard down. That's when the critical conversations start, and you can share biblical perspectives, your personal views, and your concerns for them and the world social justice is creating.

It's essential to recognize that this method has a particular form and purpose and is very effective when followed. Remember, its purpose challenges the post-truth Marxist worldview and LGBTQ ideology using the failures of its assumptions. When you ask questions that reveal the failures of the ideology, it's best to continue with them until you've finished making your point.

Be careful not to switch to using authorities in the middle of the position you're presenting, or the conversation will fall apart in a heartbeat. If you start with questions that challenge assumptions and then introduce biblical passages or your feelings about LGBTQ ideology in the middle of the conversation, you've mixed two styles of evidence and argument. The odds are you'll create conflict. Have entirely separate conversations about biblical perspectives, historical perspectives, and your positions. When you do, ask for their reaction and LISTEN, even if you don't like the answer you're hearing. If you want them to listen to you, you must listen to them.

When it comes to faith, you must practice what you preach. If most families were honest, few read the Bible and pray together throughout the week. They hope to make it to church every Sunday. This means your kids' church experience is vastly different from yours. They tolerate worship one day a week, youth group is hit or miss, and they can't wait to get back into their virtual worlds with friends who embrace social justice narratives once church is over. A growing majority of kids are disconnected from the faith their family aligns with.

See it from their perspective. They listen to sermons that don't seem to apply to the complex world of woke narratives, and parents aren't modeling the principles they hear on Sundays throughout the week. Mom and Dad don't read and pray with them on the other six days. Then, out of nowhere, Scripture is quoted as the definitive authority on all LGBTQ and social justice matters. Please hear me. I'm not saying Scripture has no authority here, but it may not have much power with them. If you want faith and God's Word to be valued by your kids when you talk with them about social justice, make sure that talking, reading, praying, and sharing with them is a consistent and essential part of the life you share.

This is a journey with your children that happens over time. Be patient and trust in the power of the questions and conversations you share with them. Remember, at the end of the day, they are rational people and wise enough to recognize that they don't want a White, heterosexual man showing up at a corporation identifying as a disabled, Black lesbian. They don't want their female friend who has been running track for three years to be obliterated by a young man identifying as a woman. And none of them would ever agree to the absurdity that one day, their child must be recognized as an animal, forcing them to accommodate and tolerate that level of delusion. The questions work. Trust the process because, in the end, truth always wins.

As I conclude this chapter, I want you to realize that this strategy works anywhere in culture. These same questions should be presented to school boards, universities, and corporate settings by your kids in their classrooms and anywhere people present social justice as sacrosanct truth immune to any question or challenge. We face the total transformation of society from a post-truth Marxist worldview with little factual basis. It's gained momentum because we were silent, and we face the upending of Western civilization and traditional America if we stay disengaged. It's time to get engaged to reclaim our communities and protect our children.

CHAPTER 5

Your Child Is a Young White (or White Adjacent) Supremacist

Your child is a young white (or white adjacent) supremacist. You probably weren't aware because your school district didn't want you to know. They didn't want you to know that critical race theory's Marxist interpretations of race and racism in America became the paradigm for every school subject, including math and science. Critical race theory (CRT) is Marxism, the deadliest ideology the modern world has ever known, adapted to American culture. Its incorporation into public school curriculums shows how thoroughly the Progressive Left has embraced Marxism as its moral consciousness. Critical race theory uses Marxist critical theory from the Frankfurt School as the paradigm for interpreting the history of race in America,[18] prescribing social justice measures as the only solutions for the difficulties minorities experience.[19] It's

---

[18] Chris Demaske, "Critical Race Theory," The First Amendment Encyclopedia, Middle Tennessee State University, last accessed on January, 10, 2023, https://mtsu.edu/first-amendment/article/1254/critical-race-theory.

[19] Autumn A. Arnett, "Analyzing the Social Justice Implications of the Critical Race Theory Debate," Diverse Issues in Higher Education, April 7, 2022, https://www.diverseeducation.com/social-justice/article/15290662/analyzing-the-social-justice-implications-of-the-critical-race-theory-debate.

becoming the primary paradigm used to comprehend the challenging intersection of race and American society in education today.

Your children won't take a class that teaches critical race theory, but its interpretation of race in America represents the core principles for every subject of your child's public education. CRT portrays an America so thoroughly corrupted by systemic racism that White America can no longer see the supremacy it protects and privilege it enjoys. Your children are young white supremacists (or white adjacent if they are minorities benefiting from white privilege), and they don't know it yet, but their eyes are opening every day they're in school. Alexander Solzhenitsyn warned us in the *Gulag Archipelago* that anything is possible in a country that becomes complacent.[20]

Why are schools teaching your children that America is a systemically racist country and that they are young white supremacists? Critical race theory has a hold on the moral consciousness of the Progressive Left. It is another example of their effort to reeducate your children to embrace a post-truth Marxist worldview. CRT has become the core paradigm for public education, teaching your children that racism and white supremacy are built into every institution of American society, corrupting every interaction in life. This racism intentionally disadvantages minorities and provides privileges to White America that they are unable or unwilling to recognize. The only way to address systemic racism is to deconstruct America's institutions and build a new society

---

[20] Aleksandr Solzhenitsyn, *The Gulag Archipelago*, Abridged (New York: Harper Perennial Modern Classics, 2007).

based on social justice guided by diversity, equity, and inclusion policies. CRT is simply Marxism applied to the American story, and it's a continuation of the persistent indoctrination of your kids with a post-truth Marxist worldview. I'll help you understand how the theory works and what you can do to protect your children. We must first explain critical race theory and how it works in society.

CRT was developed in the late eighties when Harvard intellectuals began to analyze the performance of the Black community in America nearly twenty years after the implementation of the civil rights movement and affirmative action programs. These programs were supposed to end the disparities in outcomes between Black and White America. But Harvard professors, unfortunately, recognized that decades after the programs began, Black America was still underperforming White America in every critical measure of success like education level, median income, wealth, and incarceration.[21] I'll give you an example.

When researchers compare SAT scores for Black and White high school students, Black students score about 150 to 200 points less on the SAT than White students every year. It's an outcome that's not good for Black students, the Black community, or our society.[22]

---

[21] Jelani Cobb, "The Man Behind Critical Race Theory," The New Yorker, September 20, 2021, https://www.newyorker.com/magazine/2021/09/20/the-man-behind-critical-race-theory

[22] Anna Aldric, "Average SAT Scores over Time: 1972-2021," PrepScholar, last modified October 24, 2021, https://blog.prepscholar.com/average-sat-scores-over-time.

The Black community experiences similar disparities in outcomes for nearly every critical socioeconomic factor for life in America, and Harvard intellectuals wanted to know why the differences persisted year after year. Their search for answers leads to the development of critical race theory.

The intellectuals considered three possible reasons causing disparities. The first, possible genetic differences or inferiority between races, was rejected because genetic inferiority doesn't exist. Second, cultural differences between races influence behaviors that lead to disparities, which was denied despite mountains of evidence that definitively shows that cultural experiences *significantly* influence outcomes.[23] The Harvard intellectuals chose the third possible explanation, Marxist critical theory, which presumed that systemic exploitation was built into the institutions of American society, which meant oppression and victimization in the form of systemic racism, were deeply embedded into America's social structure. Critical race theory developed when the Harvard intellectuals applied Marxist critical theory as the singular paradigm to understand the experience of minorities in America.

Critical race theory considers structural racism, racism built into the structures of American institutions, that is, slavery or Jim Crow laws, as the predominant cause of racism in America. Structural racism disadvantages minorities and privileges White America providing them with a position of supremacy over all other races. Critical race theorists refuse to consider that disparities

---

[23] Wilfred Reilly, *Taboo – 10 Facts (You Can't Talk About)* (Washington, D.C.: Regnery Publishing, 2020), 77,78.

between races in America can arise from other factors. Their singular reliance on Marxist critical theory is another example of the increasing embrace of Marxism as the moral paradigm for the Progressive Left.

It's essential to recognize that the intellectuals ignored the abundant evidence (facts and data) that cultural experiences influence an overwhelming number of the disparities minorities experience in America. Rejecting that, they embraced Marxist interpretations of American history and culture as the definitive explanation for the adverse outcomes minorities experience. CRT's incorporation into curriculums of public education is another example of the continued effort to supplant the traditional American worldview with post-truth Marxism at the expense of kids' emotional and intellectual development. Like LGBTQ ideology, you can challenge the indoctrination your kids receive with CRT principles in public schools. To protect your children, you need to understand how critical theory developed from Marxism and how it works in society.

We begin with Marxism, the philosophical and economic theories of Karl Marx. It can be complicated and convoluted, but these are the essential points you need to know about Marxism that influence your children. Marxism is a moral theory that proposes a cause for all suffering, exploitation, victimization, crime, and everything negative in our world. It also offers a means to end suffering, providing a theoretical roadmap to a utopian society, the earthly salvation of humanity. School districts present Marxism to your children as a moral theory, a superior replacement for the

Judeo-Christian worldview, and it's raging like wildfire. Here's how it's led to critical race theory and the indoctrination of your children.

Marxism places the moral responsibility for all the suffering and adverse outcomes people experience on the design of a society and its institutions. A society designed to enable exploitation and oppression creates the conditions and desires in people that make exploitation and oppression possible and profitable. In the mind of Marxists and Progressives, social institutions condition people's thoughts and actions; therefore, corrupt social institutions condition people to victimize others, continuing endless cycles of exploitation and oppression. Society's institutions control the behaviors and outcomes of people's lives. Institutions built on exploitation create suffering, while those designed on social justice and equity create a utopia. This marks a profound transformation of the way we understand morality and justice. Marxism shifts moral responsibility from individual behavior to social architecture, weaving morality and justice into the fabric of society by the design of its institutions. A new concept of justice, social justice, emerges. Social justice seeks to end human suffering by deconstructing societies built on exploitation that creates inequalities, creating new institutions designed to achieve "equity," equality of outcome for everyone.

Karl Marx felt that capitalism caused economic exploitation and inequalities responsible for humanity's real suffering. Capitalism created significant disparities in income—some attained wealth while others lived in extreme poverty. The system that benefits the rich traps the poor in endless cycles of wage slavery, where the rich steal life's resources from the poor as they achieve great wealth. In Marx's mind, this was capitalist theft, enslaving people into endless cycles of victimization and suffering that led to death. Marx proposed that capitalist economic exploitation was responsible for the entire scope of human suffering worldwide, causing every negative societal interaction and, ultimately the complete decay of society.

People were victims of exploitation built into the corrupt capitalist society. If somebody stole, it wasn't because they were thieves; they stole because economic exploitation left them starving. They were victims of wage slavery, needing to steal to survive. Alcoholics drank to deal with the pain of exploitation. Murderers killed, responding to the rage they felt reacting to victimization. People were ultimately victims of the corrupt societal institution of capitalist economics. As you can see, the victimization interpretation is endless.

For Marx, the destruction of capitalism and pursuit of economic equity (equal outcomes for all) through the institution of a communist society became an absolute moral imperative. In theory, you could eliminate all human suffering by destroying a corrupt capitalist society, replacing it with one that could achieve economic equality among all its people.

This is precisely why Marxists want to deconstruct oppressive social institutions that cause disparities and reorder them to achieve equity. They assume a ubiquitous "structural oppression" was built into the framework of institutions in society, causing endless suffering for the oppressed. Thus, they interpret every disparity that humans experience through the lens of an oppressor/

victim narrative, claiming that differences in outcomes are direct evidence of the oppression and exploitation they assume are at work. Since the structures of society bear the ultimate moral responsibility for the outcomes of humanity, whoever controls the architecture of society controls whether people live in a utopia or incomprehensible suffering. Eliminating structural oppression and exploitation by reorganizing society to conform to social justice initiatives achieves equity, ends suffering, and ultimately saves humanity. This is why social justice is the hallmark of virtue in a Marxist society.

Karl Marx felt that exploitation, oppression, and victimization were built primarily into the economic systems of capitalist societies—a privileged few gained incredible wealth while the masses suffered in horrible poverty. His later disciples, the Critical Theorists of the Frankfurt School, didn't take such a limited view that exploitation was limited to capitalist economics. They felt every aspect of Western society was corrupt and developed critical theory to expand Marxism beyond the limits of economics. Critical theorists proposed that Marx's concept of exploitation and oppression was incorporated into every aspect of Western society from its very beginning.[24] People gained power and privilege through corrupt social institutions that allowed the privileged to succeed at the expense of the oppressed. This had profound consequences for people who benefited from structural exploitation. They couldn't see the privilege they received or the suffering they

---

[24] Douglass Kellner, *Critical Theory, Marxism and Modernity* (Cambridge: Polity Press, 1989), 1-12.

caused. Exploitation became so normal to them that they could not recognize it and change. As a result, Western society was beyond repair, it needed to be deconstructed, and a new society based on equity must be built in its place.

Critical race theorists adopted Marxist critical theory to explain the reason behind disparities in outcomes between Black and White America, concluding all inequalities were the result of the inherent structural racism that was built into the architecture of America's institutions from their beginning. They presumed American society was built upon the racial exploitation, victimization, and oppression of indigenous Americans and people of color beginning as early as 1619 when the first enslaved Africans came to America. White America built racist exploitation into the structures of every American institution to provide them with a privileged position in society.[25, 26, 27] Their privileged position became so implicit (normalized and unrecognized) that White America considered their supremacy the reasonable norm. The bias was so deep that they could not see the privilege they gained through racist exploitation.

---

[25] Nicole Hannah-Jones, *The 1619 Project* (New York: Random House, 2019), large print, 8-60.

[26] The significant factual inaccuracies of *The 1619 Project* were admitted by none other than the New York Times, the work's primary sponsor. As with nearly all Marxist narratives, it is significantly disconnected from factual reality. Yet this work has become the paradigm for public school curriculums and persists as the reigning story of race in America, past and present.

[27] Post Editorial Board, "The New York Times Corrects the 1619 Project-but it's still a giant lie," New York Post, March 14, 2020, https://nypost.com/2020/03/14/new-york-times-corrects-the-1619-project-but-its-still-a-giant-lie/.

Here are the basic principles of critical race theory that are presented as sacrosanct truth to your kids within their public schools.

American society and its cultural institutions were built upon racism and the exploitation of Black and indigenous peoples. Racism is so deeply ingrained in America that every interaction in society has a racist component discriminating against minorities, no matter how benign or innocent the interaction may seem. White America receives a privileged status from this implicit, profoundly ingrained bias that it cannot recognize, thus perpetuating and protecting systemic racism. American society was constructed to protect the supremacy of White America and preserve the racist exploitation of BIPOC (Black, Indigenous, and People of Color) communities. Every member of the white community participating in American society is a white supremacist who preserves and protects the privilege of the white community. This means your child is a white supremacist (or white adjacent) regardless of their age because they happen to be white (or a minority), benefitting from a white culture that affords them a position of privilege in America. CRT calls for reorganizing America's institutions based on the diversity, equity, and inclusion paradigm. Kids are instructed to reimagine life through the lens of diversity, equity, and inclusion to recognize and address the impact of privilege. This is the paradigm for your child's public education, and the message is conveyed in narratives throughout every subject, even math and science.

We can't deny the horrors of America's racist past of slavery, Jim Crow laws, segregation, and discrimination. But America has worked to eliminate legalized discrimination from society through the civil rights movement and affirmative action program. These programs were designed to help Black communities overcome the damage caused by America's history of systemic racism and provide them with the resources and opportunities they need to succeed. The question is whether critical race theory is correct. The imprint of slavery and racism is so grievous and inescapably woven into the fabric of America's society that it's impossible to overcome with investments through legislation and social programs. Only the complete reordering of American society to achieve racial equity and the reeducation of your children to confess their privilege can bring racism to an end.

Which forces us to ask, what evidence is there for critical race theory's Marxist interpretation of American society?

Harvard intellectuals were distressed to realize the disparities between Black and White America continued twenty years after the civil rights and affirmative action movements (remember, these programs were expected to close the gap). They concluded that the persistent disparity in outcomes for the Black community was incontrovertible proof that implicit, systemic racism was so deeply embedded in the structure of society that it overwhelmed any positive effects the civil rights movement and affirmative action programs had for Black and minority communities. Today the adherents of CRT claim every disparity between Black and White America as concrete evidence that confirms the theory and are unwilling to consider other factors that could be involved.

Let's look at a few examples of CRT's interpretation of race in society. Critical race theorists claim disparities in SAT scores result from tests created by White America to benefit White students, disadvantaging minorities. The disadvantage is built into the test structure based upon the cultural bias of questions written from white cultural perspectives. CRT proponents claim racist police forces intentionally target and kill unarmed Black men at disproportionately higher rates than White men every year. Black men are deliberately removed from society when they are relentlessly profiled and targeted for arrest by racist law enforcement. A systemically racist criminal justice system intentionally sentences Black men to longer terms for drug convictions than White men who commit drug crimes. Critical race theorists claim every disparity is direct evidence of structural racism and deny cultural factors have any influence. But what do the evidence, *facts and data*, have to say? What about the mountains of evidence that show cultural factors are the main drivers of the differences in outcomes? Cultural analysis relying on facts and data paints an entirely different picture.

This is where we begin to gain the information to challenge critical race theory and the indoctrination of your children. A careful analysis of the facts and data from a cultural perspective gives us the knowledge and perspective to ask the right questions.

Highly accredited Black intellectuals analyzing the impact of cultural influences on disparities show that differences in cultural experiences drive many of the differences in outcomes. As Wilfred Reilly, a Black associate professor at the historic black college, Kentucky State University, notes in his book, *Taboo – 10 Facts (You Can't Talk About)*, quantitative scholars using linear and logistic regression analyses show that one or two cultural differences can account for disparities that are attributed to systemic, structural racism.[28] Here's what the evidence shows.

Repeated studies show that parent education and family dynamics significantly influence children's academic success, even more than race or income. Parents that achieved bachelor's and post-graduate degrees value education, passing this on to their children. These parents minimize video games, expecting their kids to study and do homework, which leads to success. When the value of hard work and learning is incorporated into the family structure, children of minority communities facing overwhelming educational barriers can achieve incredible academic success.

The profound influence of family structure and academic expectations on education success is demonstrated within the Asian immigrant community.

The academic achievements of children of Asian immigrants continue to challenge CRT's interpretation of white supremacy dominating American society and education. Asian SAT scores rank higher than White SAT scores every year.[29] Yet many Asian immigrant children face the same challenges to academic achievement that critical race theorists claim are examples of structural racism that negatively impact Black students. These include low education levels of parents, lower socio-economic status and household income, and difficulties with language and culture. Yet

---

[28] Reilly, *Taboo – 10 Facts (You Can't Talk About)*, 77,78.

[29] Anna Aldric, "Average SAT Scores over Time: 1972-2021," PrepScholar, last modified October 24, 2021, https://blog.prepscholar.com/average-sat-scores-over-time.

Asian students' SAT scores are among the highest as a group each year, overcoming barriers that CRT theorists claim are systemic racism and insurmountable by the Black community. Jennifer Lee and Min Zhou highlight the dilemma in *The Asian American Achievement Paradox*.

> "How do we explain the exceptional academic achievement of the children of Asian immigrants, including those whose parents were penniless immigrants and refugees when they arrived in the United States, having only an elementary school education, do not speak English, and who work in ethnic restaurants and factories?"[30]

It's hard to imagine a more disadvantaged minority student population or that such a group would have ANY possible pathway to success. Yet they outperform every other ethnic group in America except for one. The question is how?

Lee and Zhou argue that Asian parents and the larger Asian community have a specific "success frame," where they expect their children will earn a degree from an elite university and work in a high-status field. This frame is reinforced within the Asian community, which provides resources such as college preparation courses and tutoring to students, even their low-income members. The expectations for exceptional academic performance are

---

[30] Jennifer Lee and Min Zhou, *The Asian American Achievement Paradox* (New York: Russell Sage Foundation, 2015), 4.

extraordinarily high. Asian parents "redefined" the grade scale; in their eyes, an A- is an Asian "F." They won't accept anything less than a child's best performance. They are willing to organize their lives, household schedules, and communities so their children can take advantage of every opportunity. Asian students respond with an exceptional work ethic and are recognized as the most focused and hardworking students in their schools. Their success is attributed to families' and communities' choices that give their children the best opportunity to succeed.[31] Cultural decisions have profound impacts leading to success.

Asian immigrants aren't the only immigrant community overcoming incredible barriers, challenging CRT's Marxist narratives. African immigrants have the highest level of academic achievement among minority groups in America, surpassing White and Asian communities each year. According to recent surveys based on US Census data, African immigrants have become the "model minority community" achieving academic and professional success at rates that exceed native-born majority and minority groups. They succeed even though they were born in developing countries, predominantly live in inner-city neighborhoods, and are considered part of the Black minority community.[32] They attribute their success to the expectations and cultural fabric of African immigrant

---

[31] Review of *The Asian American Achievement Paradox*, by Jennifer Lee and Min Zhou, Google Books, June 30, 2015, https://books.google.com/books/about/The_Asian_American_Achievement_Paradox.html?id=QwZpCAAAQBAJ

[32] Serah Shani, *African Immigrant Families in the United States* (Lanham: Lexington Books, 2019) xii-xix.

communities which have expectations and family accommodations for academic success similar to the Asian immigrant community. The success of both Asian and African immigrants would be impossible if CRT's interpretation of American society were true. Their success challenges CRT's assertion that the hierarchy of white supremacy predetermines the economic and educational achievements of the Black community in America.

Family structure, not race, has the single greatest impact on the success of any child in America. Living in a single-parent family is the best predictor of a child experiencing disparities and adverse outcomes in every significant aspect of life, SAT scores included. The unfortunate fact for the Black community is that nearly 70 percent of Black households have only one parent. Fathers leave their children, which subjects kids to adverse outcomes that result from living in homes without structure and guidance.[33]

Harvard economist Roland Fryer, who won the equivalence of a Nobel Prize for Economics, has shown that an analysis of policing data does not support the narrative that police shoot Black men at disproportionately higher rates than White Americans.[34] He is not the only Black intellectual to reach the same conclusion looking at the same data. Incarceration rates for Black males are analyzed yearly to ensure that they correlate with arrest and conviction rates. Black males are incarcerated at higher rates than White males. Still, the unfortunate facts demonstrate that young

---

[33] Reily, *Taboo: 10 Facts (You Can't Talk About)*, 84-92.

[34] Fryer Jr., Roland G. 2017, "An Empirical Analysis of Racial Differences in Police Use of Force." OpenScholar@Harvard, https://scholar.harvard.edu/files/fryer/files/empirical_analysis_tables_figures.pdf.

Black males commit a higher proportion of violent and drug-related crime yearly, even though they comprise a small fraction of the overall American population. Their incarceration rates match arrest and conviction records, and no police or criminal justice department in America in recent times has policies that intentionally target minorities for arrest and incarceration, deliberately removing them from communities.[35]

Critical race theorists charge that Black males are given longer sentences for drug convictions than White males. While it is true that sentences for crack cocaine, which predominates in the Black community, are longer than sentences for powder cocaine, which prevails in the White community, the harsher sentencing was requested by Black leaders because crack cocaine was having such a debilitating effect on Black communities in the 1980s and 90s. White Americans convicted for selling methamphetamine, a drug with the same use, economic characteristics, and adverse impact on communities as crack cocaine, receive sentences comparable to Black Americans convicted for selling crack.[36]

A cultural analysis paints a vastly different picture of the cause of disparities in America. There is a wealth of information from Black intellectuals like Wilford Riley, Thomas Sowell, Roland Fryer, Glenn Lowrey, Shelby Steele, Coleman Hughes, and others. It takes time to research, but the information you need to ask the right questions to challenge the post-truth Marxist indoctrination

---

[35] Reilly, *Taboo: 10 Facts (You Can't Talk About)*, 57 – 59.
[36] "Crack vs Meth" Investor's Business Daily, July, 28th, 2011, https://www.investors.com/politics/editorials/crack-vs-meth/.

of your children can be found in the books and YouTube videos of these and other exceptional Black intellectuals.

Here's how you use the information.

Use the same format we used to challenge LGBTQ ideology and ask questions that show critical race theory's failures when facts demonstrate that cultural influences almost always have the most significant impact on disparities. First, ask initial questions so you can establish the fundamental assumptions behind critical race theory embedded in the examples of inequalities between races, then follow with questions that demonstrate cultural factors drive many of the differences in outcomes between Black and White America. When your kids talk about white privilege, ask them to define it as precisely as possible. Ask them how white privilege works in society and identify the criteria they use to determine privilege. Follow with questions that challenge their positions based on facts, data, and cultural perspectives. Here's how this works with the example of SAT scores.

If they claim that the SAT is racially biased, ask them for reasons that make it biased to the advantage of White students. They'll often reply that the analytical reading and writing sections use cultural experiences and subject material familiar to White students. The verbal section favors White students by using language with which they are more familiar. Your response should involve asking questions like this, "If that's true, why do Asian students overcome the barriers to education that are attributed to systemic racism inhibiting the Black community?" "If the verbal section of the SAT is written for White students; how do Asian immigrant students raised in homes where parents don't speak English score above White students on reading comprehension and written testing?" Wait for the answer and politely ask for a response if they change the subject. It is important to reinforce that Asian students consistently overcome barriers that have always been attributed to systemic racism negatively impacting the Black community.

Ask why Black African immigrants outperform both White and Asian students when it comes to education. Ask them how the design of the SAT is structurally racist if these minority communities exceed White America year after year. Asian and Black immigrants generally outperform White Americans in nearly every area of life. Ask your kids how white privilege is ubiquitous in America if these minority communities continue to thrive over and above White America every year.

They'll charge that police are targeting and murdering unarmed Black Americans at higher rates than unarmed White Americans and that it's open season on unarmed Black males. In these cases, knowing the facts is exceptionally important. The narratives often imply that racist police kill thousands of unarmed Black men annually, but the facts don't support the narrative. *The Washington Post* tracks police shootings annually, providing statistics that are easily accessible on the paper's website. In 2021, they reported that thirty-two unarmed people were shot in America, and eight were Black.[37] Each is a tragedy, but the narrative that police departments are targeting and killing countless unarmed Black men each

---

[37] "Fatal Force," Washington Post, last visited on December 21, 2022, https://www.washingtonpost.com/graphics/national/police-shootings/.

year is not supported by the data. Police departments and district attorneys investigate every incident, filing criminal charges when necessary. Researchers analyze fatal shooting statistics yearly for evidence of racial bias, and no one has yet to produce any statistical analysis of data that demonstrates police target and kill Black Americans at higher rates than White Americans. The data does not support the claim that police specifically target and murder Black males at disproportionally higher rates when analyzed across multiple factors. Each death is a tragedy, but the narrative that it's open season on unarmed Black men for murder by police isn't supported by the statistics.

As you can see, analyzing data from a cultural perspective reveals an entirely different analysis of the cause of racial disparities in America. That's not to say that systemic racism doesn't exist, racism has been wholly purged from American society, or that we've reached a point where we no longer must be concerned about the impact of racism. The fight against racism never ends. But this analysis demonstrates the Progressive Left's complete embrace of Marxist narratives as their defining moral paradigm and disregard for the reality that a rational analysis of the facts shows. Marxist theory dictates the narrative, meaning critical race theory principles must be imposed upon your kids as sacrosanct truth without being challenged. Our schools have been happy to comply. They forgot they're dealing with parents. We refuse to. We push back.

Remember, it's all about the questions. The challenge is getting your kids to think about the complex factors that influence disparities in America and the picture that facts, data, and cultural perspectives present. You want to ask questions that force your child to open within the assumptions they've received through the indoctrination that America is an inherently racist society that intentionally disadvantages minorities and privileges White people in ways White people cannot see. It's important not to let your child pivot away from the information challenging them. Your kids won't like the facts, but don't let them run. If you give them information about cultural influences driving the differences in SAT scores and they choose to pivot the conversation away, gently bring them back. Ask them to provide you with an answer to a reasonable question. Let this process take time. You're not trying to force them to see a new perspective immediately; you're giving them information that will challenge them to consider what the facts have to say about race in America.

Facts and truth have consistently revealed the failure of indoctrination. There is a significant body of fact-based evidence provided by Black intellectuals that you can use to present information that challenges the principles of CRT. There is a wealth of information on YouTube. Search for videos provided by the Black intellectuals I listed and begin listening. It might seem unclear to start, but once you connect with their thoughts, things will begin to make sense. Remember that the more factual evidence you have, the better. Ultimately, we are attempting to accurately assess race and culture in America. Challenging the narratives of CRT is not stating or implying that systemic racism doesn't exist anywhere in America. Traditional Americans are willing to work tirelessly to end any systemic racism written into our institutions' laws and programs. Post-truth Marxists are unwilling to embrace anything beyond their Marxism.

If you're willing to go deeper, you can explain the Marxist roots of critical race theory and its implications for our society. Anti-racist scholars like Ibram X. Kendi make no effort to hide their Marxist interpretations of race in America. That's truly frightening when one considers Marxism, the deadliest ideology the modern world has ever known. During the twentieth century, Marxists murdered over one hundred million people to pursue a utopian society within the former Soviet Union, communist China, Vietnam, Cambodia, and Cuba. Although we will never know the true total, the official Soviet estimate of the number of deaths occurring in their concentration camps is sixty-six million.[38] It's estimated that Mao Zedong murdered a minimum of forty-eight million people in China during the Great Leap Forward, with most of these deaths occurring from 1958 to 1962.[39] These aren't the only examples of Marxist genocide and they should immediately disqualify every aspect of Marxism and the post-truth Marxist worldview. Yet the embrace of Marxism continues. Kids need to know that this genocidal ideology has become the paradigm for their public education, but few among us are aware.

I often challenge students with this perspective. We've worked hard to educate about the horrors of Nazi ideology because of the genocide of six million Jews in the Holocaust, removing the

---

[38] Solzhenitsyn, *The Gulag Archipelago*, 178.

[39] Didi Kirsten Tatlow, "A Great Leap into the Abyss," The New York Times, September 5, 2012, https://www.nytimes.com/2012/09/06/world/asia/06iht-letter06.html.

ideology's influence within our culture. Yet few people in America are even aware of the magnitude of the genocide committed by Marxists when they applied Marxist theory to achieve their theoretical utopia. Marxists perfected the use of concentration camps to murder and silence opposition long before the Nazis in Germany. Their cruelty and barbaric behavior far surpass anything that happened in the Third Reich. Take a moment to research Cannibal Island in the Soviet Union, Mao's "Great Leap Forward" in China, and the Killing Fields of Cambodia. Marxist societies murdered over one hundred million people who refused to comply with social justice measures in their countries. The estimates have never been disputed by the regimes that perpetrated this genocide. It's the ultimate cancel culture. Here's a question I often ask, "If we universally disqualify Nazi ideology because of the six million deaths in the Holocaust, how can we engage any form of Marxism, including critical race theory, if Marxism murdered over one hundred million?" It's a question everyone needs to consider.

This strategy works, but it takes longer for some kids than others, and you need to be prepared to support your kids as they come to terms with the questions. Challenging social justice narratives isn't a simple intellectual process for kids. Disengaging from woke culture means they'll have to break from their social circles, which means the threat of cancel culture. Social cancelation is one of their biggest challenges and a big hurdle for them to overcome. Woke teachers refuse to accept perspectives that don't walk in lockstep with social justice narratives, and "friends" are more than eager to exact social punishments on kids who refuse to embrace the indoctrination without question.

The message is loud and clear: conform or be cast out, and you'll need to be there for them to get them through.

CHAPTER 6
Conform or Be Cast Out

Cancel culture is the enforcement arm of the post-truth Marxist movement and ensures maximum compliance to the indoctrination your children receive. It won't tolerate challenges to the post-truth Marxist worldview and has a long list of coercive punishments ready and waiting for anyone who bucks the system. It's conform or be cast out for your kids. This follows the long deadly history of the Marxist tradition, where even the most minor acts of noncompliance within Marxist societies resulted in imprisonment and often death in a concentration camp. It shouldn't be surprising that post-truth Marxists are willing to exact even the most extreme social punishment on noncompliant children today. There is a method to this madness; it's purely by design.

For Marxists, the highest form of moral virtue happens when people conform to the demands of societies designed to achieve equity through social justice. Morality and virtue are achieved by conforming to society's rules, not by the moral refinement of individual character. Marxist societies can only be successful when everyone agrees to work together collectively to achieve equity, equal outcomes, among all members of society. Individualism leads to people determining their success, which invariably creates inequalities; some have more, and others have less, which is direct evidence of exploitation. That's why cancel culture punishes those who step out of line. Social justice can't work unless everyone agrees to work together to achieve equity and end inequalities.

It's essential to understand why equity is the ultimate measure of moral virtue for Marxists and why achieving it is so important. Equity is equality of outcome, which means that every member of society experiences equal levels of success; it's the ultimate protection against oppression, victimization, and exploitation. When everyone agrees to equal outcomes, it eliminates a person's ability to maximize their success, which can create inequalities when people achieve far more than others. In Marx's mind, inequality is evidence of exploitation, victimization, and oppression, which leads to crime, poverty, famine, war, and murder. A world that achieves equity, equal outcomes for its people, eliminates inequalities and the human suffering they cause. This amounts to the world's salvation—in theory, a utopian society should emerge. Nothing will stand in their way; it's convert or die, conform or be cast out. Over one hundred million people lost their lives refusing to conform to Marxist ideologies. Your children are caught in the struggle.

When your children embrace concepts of liberty and freedom of traditional America, they represent a major obstacle, blocking the path to the future of post-truth Marxism. America has always prized the protection of liberty and the right for individuals to define their destiny as the highest ideal for humanity. The

Founding Fathers wanted only minimal and necessary restrictions on human freedom as they were required to maintain an ordered society. But liberty comes with specific opportunities and risks. Freedom allows some to achieve far more than others based on their skills and merit. It runs the risk of creating inequalities that cause exploitation, oppression, and victimization when some choose to take advantage of others. Marxists attribute all that is evil in the world to the abuse of achievement that can happen when people are given the right to self-determination. In a post-truth Marxist world, freedom and liberty are the antitheses of conformity to social justice that leads to equity. As a protector of these virtues, American society must be deconstructed if Marxism is going to save the world. Your children are pawns in the game.

Let's talk about how cancel culture operates in your kids' lives.

In America, post-truth Marxists use cancelation through socialization pressure and ostracization to enforce compliance with social justice narratives by punishing people when they don't. High school students that have bought into social justice narratives can be vicious when kids refuse to conform. Your child's "friends" will turn on them when they begin to question social justice narratives. The attacks are astonishing—kids get ejected from social circles and cut off from relationships. They are labeled racists, Nazis, homophobic fascists, transphobic haters, and threatened with physical violence. I've witnessed this in action, and it's stunning to realize that we've come to a place in America where there's no longer room for free speech or counter perspectives based on facts and reason. Social media gives bullies a broad reach to punish, and kids who reject social justice narratives find themselves at odds with entire student bodies. Kids don't simply lose a circle of friends; everyone knows in their classes, sports teams, clubs, and school buses. Kids who speak their minds know it's impossible to hide—cancel culture and social media reach every area of life.

This preys on one of the most critical aspects of your young teen's mind: the desire to gain peer acceptance and belong to social groups. It's one of the most significant influences in your child's life; participating in social relationships is the same as breathing air for them. Most of their relating happens through social media, which has become a toxic playground for kids' hearts and minds. NYU professor Jonathan Haidt has raised the alarm about the devastating effects "normal" social media use has on children's mental health and wellness. Current rates of anxiety, mental health issues, and suicide for teens under social media influence have risen to levels that exceed the threshold for a national health crisis.[40, 41] That's social media's power over kids, even under the "best" circumstances. When it's used to punish non-conformity, it becomes an even more powerful tool. Here's why.

Socialization pressure and peer interaction are the most important influences in your kids' lives. The phones give them continuous access to social groups—they spend far more time interacting with them than anyone else. More and more teens

---

[40] Jonathan Haidt provides an extensive list of resources documenting the negative effects of social media on adolescent mental health at the following link.

[41] "Social Media," Jonathan Haidt, last accessed December 27, 2022, https://jonathanhaidt.com/social-media/.

tell researchers that their relationships with peers are far more important than their relationships with their parents. The difference in the amount of time kids spend talking with peers versus the time they spend communicating with parents is astounding. Kids living in two-parent homes are busy with after-school activities, sports, homework, and video games. They may live under your roof, but they're busy doing other things; they aren't having conversations and building relationships with you.

Living in the same house isn't the same as having direct conversations and communication with your children. Most parents spend less than ten hours a week of direct dialogue with their kids, discussing a wide variety of subjects that may not include concerns about social justice. Kids see their peers all day in school and spend additional hours connecting through text and social media, which adds up to about thirty to forty hours per week. Many kids say their peers are more important than their parents. Non-stop communication with peers is their emotional life. They can't comprehend being cast out of social groups, making the pressure to conform to social justice narratives almost beyond comprehension. Stepping outside the lines destroys their entire world, and they know it.

Conformity to social justice narratives brings social acceptance; it's their emotional currency, and kids will choose social acceptance over reality. They intuitively recognize that high school boys are destroying girls' track events, peers identify as cats, and white privilege can't pass intellectual scrutiny. But they are unwilling to face cancelation and become ostracized from their social groups, so they conform. It's a vicious cycle that's hard to break but can be broken. Here's how to do it.

You start by building connections and trust with your kids, so you are a refuge when they get canceled and cast out. Their worlds fall apart when they buck the system, and they have to rely on you to support them as they rebuild their lives. This is where the relationship-building and trust you built by doing the things they enjoy bears fruit. As parents, you have an advantage over phones and social media. The virtual world can't take the place of interacting with a parent who loves them. This might sound trite, but it has immense value. Start by setting time aside each week to do things they want to do together. Ask them what they are interested in (don't bring your list, asking them to do what you like).

Get emotionally invested with them, especially if it moves you out of your comfort zone. This is critical. Let the activity be about spending time with them, and don't make it a front for a conversation to challenge social justice issues. They'll know if it's happening naturally. They'll disconnect if they see you using time together as a vehicle for talks with an agenda. Make your relationship a priority, ultimately bringing more value than their peers. It takes time, but it will happen. Your relationship is your bond. I hope your marriage and your children become the most important relationships based on the time you spend together. Consider counseling with your children if your relationships are strained. They can be rebuilt, and you can reconnect.

This journey isn't about information; it's about your ability to communicate with your kids, which depends on the level of trust and connection they have with you. If you want to protect them, invest in your relationship with them, and realize that acquiring the intellectual tools to challenge the indoctrination will have little impact if you can't connect. It's essential because they need to know they can trust YOU to be their support system, a relationship they can count on as they reorder their world. When they get canceled and bullied, they need to look to you as a support to help guide them through the process.

Here are tools you can use to help your kids through the journey. Use cancel culture against itself. Asking questions is exceptionally effective during the cancelation. Once my oldest son made up his mind, he broke from the pack almost overnight, and the retribution was astounding. As painful as this was, the entire process revealed the agenda of cancel culture and the post-truth Marxist world, and I used every moment to help him.

When kids get canceled, their worlds collapse almost overnight. One minute they are caught up in the constant texting on Snapchat with friends, and in an instant, they're under assault with no one to talk to. They lose long-term friendships and are attacked by kids they hardly know, wondering what it will be like in the halls and locker room. They transition from an ordered world to chaos at the speed of social media, which means they have no one to talk to and no one to connect with. They'll smile, act normal, and might share a little, but odds are they'll suffer in silence through an electronic war that's happening on their phone. As a parent, you must understand that this happens virtually, which means you'll know almost nothing they're experiencing. Kids will try to keep it inside, but it will bleed out over time, and you have to be prepared to be there for them when they do.

This is where the relationship-building that you've done together pays off. When I realized what was happening with my son, I made sure I was there to fill the void when cancel culture collapsed his world. We spent a lot of time together, from practicing baseball to getting food and watching football. I found he'd come to me for conversations he would have had with the "friends" who canceled him. I'd drive him to get together with kids who shared the same values as he made new friendships. I made sure I was available for him, especially in the early days when the void was the largest. Eventually, he rebuilt his world and chose to attend a private Catholic high school to be surrounded by like-minded people who shared our faith.

Our time together led to some of our most important conversations in this journey. I only had to ask a couple of questions for him to understand that free speech, truth based on facts, and room for different opinions didn't exist in a woke world. His "friends" weren't friends; he was only accepted if he fully complied with woke narratives. Once he realized his public education was a form of indoctrination, he said, "Dad, I can't do this anymore. I'm never going back. I need to go to school somewhere else." He's never looked back. His brother graduated from public school, and I continue challenging social justice narratives with him. He's a math and science kid who sees the narratives as a profound waste of time and mental energy. I continue to track with him weekly, spending time in conversations whenever issues arise. I'm proud to watch him engage facts with rational thought and embrace conclusions that break from conformist groupthink. It's a struggle, and I'm always listening to him, tracking his views, and looking for opportunities for conversation. That's why our time together is my priority.

Make sure you use every legal process to enforce boundaries on social media and cancelation. Currently, schools and police departments end online bullying immediately after it's revealed. Speaking from experience, police departments can step in to end online harassment. When parents get a phone call from law enforcement and find out their kids are bullies, they immediately stop it. If they ignore law enforcement and continue, charges can be filed. Consider using appropriate legal action if necessary and be prepared to use every available resource.

Watching your kids get canceled is hard, but it reveals many of the failures of social justice narratives for them. Nothing shouts indoctrination louder for a kid than getting attacked by their "friends" because they've adopted a reasonable counter perspective after they analyzed facts with critical thinking. It's an eye-opener for kids and parents. It's hard for all of us to comprehend how deep these shifts in philosophy and ideas are fundamentally transforming our culture. Concepts seem esoteric until drag queens and cancel culture open our eyes. Let's be honest here; we all laughed at philosophy and philosophers through the years, but philosophy matters, ideas matter, and it's time to recognize that we need a new perspective on the challenges we face.

CHAPTER 7

Perspectives

If you ask a committed post-truth Marxist about their embrace of post-truth Marxism, they'll likely look at you like you've lost your mind. They won't have a clue what post-truth Marxism is, which isn't surprising. Most of us are unaware of the moral paradigms we use to decide what is acceptable and how we organize society's institutions. People have little knowledge of philosophy; they work from a sense of what seems or feels right to them without asking why they embrace their values or how they decide what's acceptable for our culture. Most people are unaware that significant philosophical revolutions completely transform how people perceive their world. These shifts happen slowly over time, taking generations to transform culture, and people change slowly along with them.

These quiet revolutions change how people decide what's right, regardless of whether they realize they're part of a significant philosophical transformation reordering society. That is a critical point that's important for us to understand. People don't experience worldview changes through technical discussions about philosophy; they experience them as shifts in how they perceive what's right for the world, agreeing with ideas and movements without knowing why. This vehicle brings all of these profound cultural changes to your children's classrooms. Their teachers and administrators have caught a radical new vision of the woke world of diversity and equity drifting through academia and culture, which seems to them like a vast improvement on the "failures" of America. They want to change the world according to their vision, starting with changing your kids. It's essential to understand how these complex ideas transform our society.

Most people don't know what postmodernity is, let alone any one principle that defines the movement, but they'll agree with a postmodern worldview when it manifests itself in society. This is precisely how this operates in your child's school. Your child's teacher may not know the core principles of postmodernity, but they are confident that truth is not objective; everyone has their perspective and can determine what is right or wrong for themselves. The story of American exceptionalism is a myth that leads to oppression, and rational thought is not the only way to perceive "reality." When they embrace the world from these points of view, they are genuinely postmodern without knowing any of the technical points of postmodern philosophy. Their intuition tells them this is the correct perspective on the world without knowing why. Intellectual revolutions happen to us whether we realize it or not; this is precisely what's happening with the emergence of post-truth Marxism.

I can't point to a group of philosophers presenting this as formal epistemology, a theory of knowledge. My analysis here is purely observational; I call what I see. People are creating a new moral paradigm on the fly out of necessity without really being aware of the intellectual transformations they are embracing. Post-truth Marxism fulfills the intellectual vacuum left by postmodernity as the West breaks away from the influence of rational thought and Judeo-Christianity. Teachers won't verbalize this, nor do they even comprehend what is happening. Post-truth Marxism offers people an intellectual justification to create the world they want; it just feels right to them in the absence of Judeo-Christianity's influence.

That's the driving force for a post-truth culture. People don't know philosophy; they resonate with the society it creates. If you challenge your child's teacher about their post-truth orientation, they'll look at you like you've lost your mind. But every Kindergarten Drag Queen Story Hour, gender unicorn, and gender equity workshop they inflict upon your kids demonstrate their embrace of post-truth. They don't care about philosophy. If you bring it up, they'll dismiss it. Their internal moral compass tells them they must free society from traditional morality's oppression to become more open, tolerant, and inclusive. When schools promote LGBTQ ideology and the tolerance of the ever-expanding concepts of gender and sexual identity, they embrace post-truth without directly recognizing it. They take a similar approach to Marxism.

If you tell your kids' woke teachers that they are Marxists, they'll look at you like you disqualified yourself from having rational thoughts. You've instantly placed yourself in the lunatic fringe. Marxism is a loaded term most people associate with the now-defunct Soviet Union or long-dead Latin American dictators. People don't know what it is, so it's functionally disconnected from reality. Your child's teacher probably doesn't understand Marxism, but they resonate with Marxism's analysis that America's history and social institutions are corrupt. They are proud of their unqualified embrace of CRT, the district diversity, equity, and inclusion (D. E. I.) policy, and social justice initiatives. Yet, they are unaware that these are different manifestations of Marxist ideology. School districts all over the country proudly present them as proof of their Progressive "accreditation." Once again, people resonate with the society philosophy creates without ever knowing the ideas that make them. This time they are dealing with variants of Marxism, the deadliest ideology the modern world has ever known.

The bottom line here is that people are getting what they want in the short term: freedom from a traditional American worldview that embraces Judeo-Christianity's emphasis on personal virtue grounded in biblical principles. But people should be careful what they wish for. There are hidden costs buried within post-truth Marxism that Progressive Leftists seem willing to ignore, but we all might have to pay.

Post-truth allows people to affirm what they want and have what they want to be established in society. This circle of mutual tolerance allows everyone to create their preferred lifestyle without question or restriction. It's an enticing way to view the world. This enticing view is the driving force behind the Progressives using post-truth to determine "reality." It's the ultimate perspective enabling humanity's quest for complete freedom in a journey of self-fulfillment. Biblical morality is challenging, requiring the denial of the unbridled pursuit of pleasure; dying to oneself and carrying crosses puts an end to the agendas of self-gratification. Post-truth frees American society from the constraints of biblical Christianity, creating a world that affirms every desire where the only thing people deny is denial. A word to the wise, societies that have limitless freedom ultimately implode.

Post-truth works well, rescuing sexual identity and gender from the repressive "bigotry" of traditional America, but it opens Pandora's box that it can't shut. America was willing to tolerate the expansion of sexual identity and sexual expression when people promised that whatever happened between consenting adults in the privacy of their spaces stayed there. Conservative America gave ground on sexuality because, at the time, the demands didn't overturn the social order. There were decades of a live-and-let-live tolerance between Christians, Conservatives, Independents, Liberals, Progressives, and the LGB community living in tension under a traditional American social structure as postmodernity deconstructed American society and post-truth demolished every boundary.

When the rest of the identity politics special interest groups realized they could capitalize on the shifting post-truth landscape to justify their preferred self-expressions, they began the destruction of the traditional American social structure. The trans community deconstructed the traditional architecture of gender when it demanded unqualified acceptance of the gender-fluid world and complete access to any public space it wanted. The furries and minor attracted persons realized they could demand legitimacy and their piece of the new cultural real estate based on post-truth social conditioning. Every lifestyle was fair game. The lid was off Pandora's box, exposing a nasty little secret. If post-truth allows us to affirm what we want and have what we want to be affirmed, then every emotionally established position gets a seat at the table. This creates a cultural spiral where personal delusions become public realities. G. K. Chesterton warned people about taking down any fence before they knew its purpose. Be careful what you wish for; you might get it.

Merriam-Webster defines delusions as "persistent false belief regarding the self or persons or objects outside the self that is maintained despite indisputable evidence to the contrary."[42] Facts, data, and rational thought have challenged delusion with undeniable evidence to keep it bound within the realm of the personal psyche, preventing it from creating endless havoc throughout society. When the postmodern movement exiled logic and rational thought, it removed society's time-honored mechanism to challenge personal preferences, preventing them from becoming public policy. Imagine a world without reasonable challenges where people are forced to accept anything anyone wants to be based on the endless reciprocal affirmation of individual emotions and desires. The Progressive Left resists

---

[42] *Merriam-Webster Dictionary,* "delusion, n." accessed January 10, 2023, https://www.merriam-webster.com/dictionary/delusion.

any challenges to the furries using facts and rational thought; their delusions and litter boxes can become our realities.

The Progressive Left gets what it wants in the short term but is unwilling or unable to see what they set in motion. They gained the freedom for self-determination they wanted when they banished Judeo-Christian influences from the land, but they made a Faustian bargain with the rest of the world in the process. Post-truth justifications for personal self-determination aren't limited to preferred identity politics communities of gender and sexual identity. Everyone and I mean everyone, gets a seat at this table and can demand to play the game, which includes identity groups that we collectively despise, with positions that horrify us all. Imagine your worst nightmare identity group demanding legitimacy based on their emotional preferences and community affirmation. Anyone can justify any set of preferred behaviors under these rules.

Adopting Marxism and social justice is another step in the radical departure from the Judeo-Christian paradigm of traditional America. Traditional America attempts to construct a "just" society by creating virtuous individuals living by biblical justice principles. Individuals were primarily responsible for their success or failure, relying on their abilities and desire to make the best from available resources and opportunities. Fairness in traditional American society was defined by ensuring everyone had equal access to resources and opportunities. Your success or failure depended on your ability to stay focused and disciplined, to gain the skills and abilities that would allow you to succeed in a free market. This was a manifestation of the Judeo-Christian worldview that championed a life of self-control and self-discipline to grow one's talents and abilities, and it's the defining characteristic that made Western society.

The embrace of Marxism by the Progressive Left threatens to change the architecture of equality of opportunity in American society, which has been the key to its unique history. America has always attributed its success to its people applying the skills and merit of their abilities. We ensure that everyone has an equal opportunity to maximize their potential. We're a nation that values individual achievement, believing that every sum of individual exceptionalism (however realized for every person) produces an exceptional society and government. America was built on the efforts of people who strive to be the best they can be (this does not imply that America is perfected in any way). We know of no other societal architecture that's benefitted more people in more countries worldwide.

Marxist equity challenges this paradigm, inverting it and calling personal achievement criminal behavior that causes inequalities. Equity believes in ensuring equal outcomes for people regardless of their investment in their development or the application of their abilities in society. Social justice forces people to place the pursuit of equity over accomplishment, which means outcomes are defined by the limits of social justice, not by the investment someone places into their personal development or achievement. Marxism views personal achievement as criminal behavior when individual accomplishments create inequalities that theoretically drive exploitation and oppression. This must not be dismissed; Marxists ALWAYS criminalize the virtue that built America into the exceptional yet flawed society it has become. They pursue social justice without considering the consequences of replacing individual achievement with the assured outcomes of equity. They overlook the facts of history as it repeats itself over the last century.

Marxism ALWAYS fails, producing economic disaster and endless corpses. The fact that they continue to impose this failure upon unsuspecting societies is incomprehensible to anyone but Marxists themselves. Imagine, if you will, a society that kills the goose that lays its golden eggs and declares that the slaughter of the goose was the pinnacle of human virtue as it feasts off the carcass after its roasting. The Progressive Left may bask in their euphoria as Marxism achieves diversity, equity, and inclusion for the furries, MAPs, LGBTQ, and BIPOC communities. Still, they ignore that they've made yet another Faustian bargain in the process. They ignore the consequences when a society replaces individual achievement with the pursuit of equity. History reveals that equity always fails, replacing freedom and prosperity with suffering and poverty. The Progressive Left made a deal with the worst devil the modern world has ever known when they purged Judeo-Christianity from American social architecture, replacing it with Marxism. Like every generation of Marxists before them, they ignore Marxism's murderous history and are convinced that they are the generation that will bring forth the utopia.

Your kid's teachers and school district administration know none of this. They have little exposure to or understanding of the actual realities of Marxism. They're simply embracing the narrative of an America that is a racist, homophobic, transphobic, patriarchal, and xenophobic society by design. It needs to become more inclusive, embracing LGBTQ ideology, critical race theory, and other minority identity politics groups to end oppression, making America fairer and more equitable. It's an alluring idea. Who doesn't want America to be a more open, accessible, and tolerant society? But when they advance the narrative, they're embracing Marxism, whether they know it or not, presenting it to our children as a moral framework superior to the traditional American worldview. A growing number of districts exclude all counter perspectives in their zeal to advance the ideological revolution. It's classic indoctrination.

As I bring our journey to an end, I need to write that my rejection of the post-truth Marxist worldview does not in any way imply that systemic racism or oppression has never happened or can never happen in America. Or the disparities and inequalities in America are an unfortunate but acceptable reality of Western society. They aren't. We must find solutions to end the challenges disadvantaged communities face in America. Neither is it acceptable to treat the LGBTQ community with disrespect as we stridently disagree with the ideological position. I am resolutely rejecting the Marxist narratives that declare disparities and inequalities result singularly from American society's "oppressive" structure, ignoring the abundant evidence that cultural factors play an overwhelming role in creating the outcomes individuals experience. I also reject the narrative that refusing to accept every socially affirmed lifestyle without question is a form of hatred, oppression, and violence.

We have been complacent, silent for far too long, and giving up too much cultural ground.

My deep concern for the cultural divide grows daily; I don't see a way forward if people continue their indifference toward the current trends. People are angry but still disengaged, and most don't even know who is running for school boards in the next election. Our emotional outpouring of outrage is insufficient for the times. We must recognize that anger is not the same as attending school board meetings to challenge indoctrination. Our paradigms must shift from voicing our outrage to running for school boards and organizing parent groups. The days of practical engagement are here.

Marxism and traditional America have never been able to coexist in any space anywhere in the world. I can't envision that within the confines of America itself. I won't try to predict the future beyond stating the obvious. The polarization of America only grows between two sides that have fought one another on battlefields worldwide. Don't expect a reconciliation any time soon.

Please spend time thinking about these closing thoughts. As I began writing, I was determined to take you on this intellectual journey because I wanted you to understand the significance of all the transitions occurring around us. So much is at stake; our worldview and social order are contested in a cold, cultural civil war. Decades ago, intellectuals warned that Western society was at risk if the influence of postmodernity continued. As hard as it is to comprehend, it's a real possibility, now more than ever. We stand to face these challenges, not only for our kids but for America, our Judeo-Christian worldview, and Western civilization.

If you are looking for more resources for the spiritual and intellectual battle we wage, please visit my Battleground Ideas website (www.battlegroundideas.com), where you can find the video series, *How Do I Talk to my Kids about Social Justice*, which you can share. You will also find resources from various intellectuals that provide facts, data, and information that you can use in dialogue with your children and school boards. Remember, the battle belongs to the Lord, but He expects us to get up and get active in the fight for our kids, communities, and nation.

Blessings . . .

Printed in the USA
CPSIA information can be obtained
at www.ICGtesting.com
JSHW020435231123
52531JS00001B/40